THE NEW
DICTIONARY of NEEDLEPOINT & CANVAS STITCHES

Other Books by Rhoda Ochser Goldberg

The New Knitting Dictionary
The New Crochet Dictionary
The New Quilting and Patchwork Dictionary
The New Dictionary of Quilt Designs in Cross-Stitch
Needlepoint Patterns for Signs and Sayings (with Marion Pakula)

THE NEW
DICTIONARY of
NEEDLEPOINT &
CANVAS STITCHES

RHODA OCHSER GOLDBERG

BASICS • TOOLS AND ACCESSORIES • YARNS AND
THREADS • NEEDLES • MEASUREMENTS • BARGELLO •
FINISHING TOUCHES • ALPHABETS

CROWN TRADE PAPERBACKS • NEW YORK

This book is lovingly dedicated to my husband, George, without whose love, cooperation, and moral support it could not have been written.

Published by Crown Publishers, Inc., 201 East 50th Street, New York, New York 10022. Member of the Crown Publishing Group.

Random House, Inc. New York, Toronto, London, Sydney, Auckland

Crown Trade Paperbacks and colophon are trademarks of Crown Publishers, Inc.

Manufactured in the United States of America

Library of Congress Cataloging-in-Publication Data

Goldberg, Rhoda Ochser.
    The new dictionary of needlepoint and canvas stitches : basics, tools and accessories, yarns and threads, needles, measurements, bargello, finishing touches, alphabets/by Rhoda Ochser Goldberg.
        p.   cm.
    Includes index.
    1. Embroidery—Dictionaries. 2. Canvas embroidery—Dictionaries.
    I. Title.
    TT770.G63   1994
    746.44'2—dc20   93-21240
                                                                                      CIP

ISBN 0-517-88145-4

10 9 8 7 6 5 4 3 2 1

First Edition

Cover (*clockwise from top left*): Dale's Stitching Lady; Eyelet, Six-Sided; Squash Racquet Case; and Woven Ribbons.

CONTENTS

Acknowledgments   vii

Introduction   ix

THE BASICS   1
Tools and Accessories   1
Canvas   8
Plastic Canvas   9
Yarns and Threads   11

Needles   13
Measurements   14
Vocabulary   14
Bargello   16

THE STITCH DICTIONARY "A TO Z"   23

PROJECTS   161
Belt   161
Camera Case with Strap   162
Dale's Stitching Lady   165
Eyeglass Case   166
First Aid Box   168
Flask Cover   170
Jewelry/Tool Case   171
Key Chain/Identification Tag   173
Luggage Rack   174
Picture of George   176

Pocket   176
Sneaker Key/Coin Holder   178
Soda/Beer Can Cover   180
Squash or Badminton Racquet
  Case   182
Tennis Racquet Cover   184
Tennis Equipment Wall Rack   185
Tissue Box Cover   187
Visor   188

FINISHING TOUCHES   190
Care and Finishing   190

ALPHABETS   191

COLOR PHOTOGRAPHS   follows 22

Bibliography   193

Index of Stitches   194

ACKNOWLEDGMENTS

I gratefully acknowledge the support and assistance I received from my friends and family and the wonderful group of stitchers who gave so freely of their time and talents. I could not have produced a book of this scope and size without the help of these dedicated men and women.

I must thank the members and officers of the Suffolk County Chapter and the Long Island Chapter of the Embroiderers' Guild of America, the Canvas Fanatics Chapter of the American Needlepoint Guild, and a group of women from the Dix Hills Chapter of Hadassah for making the majority of the samples photographed for inclusion in this book.

A special thank you must be given to my friend Dale Sokolow for her help in suggesting stitchers, correcting instructions, stitching samples, and, most important, offering a helping hand and heart during a most difficult time in my life.

A word of gratitude to the people of the needlecraft industry who gave of their time, knowledge, equipment, and products needed to make the samples for this book. They provided the best tools, equipment, accessories, canvas, threads, and yarns. This book could not have been written without their cooperation and assistance.

I will never write a book without acknowledging the friendship of my first writing partner and teacher, Marion Pakula. Again, I thank you, Marion, for getting me started and teaching me the "ropes."

The photographs were provided by my friend Marilyn Lehrfeld. Your "eye" and photographic ability never cease to place me in awe of you. Thanks again, Marilyn.

The most important thank you goes once again to my editor, Brandt Aymar. He did his usual assisting and hand-holding, but most of all he trusted and stayed with me during the extended period of time it took to finish this book.

SAMPLES WERE MADE BY THE FOLLOWING STITCHERS:

Roberta Ast, New City, New York
Roberta Bagno, New City, New York
Larry Berger, Northport, New York
Florence Booy, Bay Shore, New York
Lynn Bryan, Kings Park, New York
Regina Bye, Bayside, New York
Jacqui Clarkson, Rockaway, New Jersey
Keith Clarkson, Rockaway, New Jersey
Liz Stewart Eannaccone, Huntington, New York
Jeanette Eisenmesser, Smithtown, New York
Helen Fey, Huntington, New York
Cynthia Forman, Flushing, New York
Janet Gerstman, Dix Hills, New York
Gloria Gralla, Flushing, New York
Carol Kempner, Brooklyn, New York
Linda Kent, New City, New York
Marilyn Klein, New Hempstead, New York

Rita Limback, Whitestone, New York
Zeena MacLean, Croton-on-Hudson, New York
Anita Miller, Boca Raton, Florida
Carole Miller, Dix Hills, New York
Jacqui O'Connell, Pensacola, Florida
Marianne Pletcher, Huntington, New York
Karen Ranlett, Evans, Georgia
Marjorie Rogers, Sayville, New York
Marcia Schulman, Smithtown, New York
Dale Sokolow, Melville, New York
Rhoda Stein, Shrub Oak, New York
Margaret Vickary, Smithtown, New York
Joyce Weinstein, East Northport, New York
Hedda Wohllebe, Dix Hills, New York
Kathleen Wolter, Dix Hills, New York
Jane Zorn, Smithtown, New York

Materials and supplies for making the samples were generously provided by the following companies:

Ben Franklin, 42 Indian Head Road, Kings Park, New York 11754 (*This is a wonderful retail source for needlework supplies, threads, and accessories. The plastic canvas was provided by this store.*)

Berroco, Uxbridge, Massachusetts (*supplied the Handeze® therapeutic gloves*)

Dal-Craft, Inc., Tucker, Georgia (*supplied the LoRan® threaders, accessory kits, and magnetic boards*)

DMC® Corporation, South Kearney, New Jersey (*all the DMC® Floralia® 3-ply Persian wool and perle cotton*)

Dritz® Corporation, Spartanburg, South Carolina (*all the Fray Check® used for samples*)

Frame Center Inc., 73 East Main Street, Smithtown, New York 11787 (*a retail source for ready-made and custom frames, mats, and all professional mounting and framing services*)

gingher® INC., Greensboro, North Carolina (*all the scissors used in the photographs to prepare the samples. This firm manufactures a complete line of precision cutting instruments for sewing, embroidery, and quilting.*)

Judi & Co., Dix Hills, New York (*all the ⅛" Starlight and ¼" ribbons used for the bargello samples*)

Kreinik Mfg., Inc., Parkersburg, West Virginia (*all the silk gauze, Siltex®, gold braids, metallic threads, 14K- and platinum-plated needles*)

Marie Products®, Tucson, Arizona (*all wood stretcher strips and bars, scroll frames, Rocky Giraffe floor stand, Easy Blocker, and Spray 'N Block™ used to make the samples*)

Susan Bates® Inc., Chester, Connecticut (*all Anchor® embroidery floss, Anchor® Tapisserie [tapestry yarn], tapestry needles #18, #22, #24 used to make the samples*)

Threadneedle Street, Five Thorman Lane, Huntington, New York 11743, (516) 427-6488 (*all major brands of yarns and fibers, canvas, and accessories. Many hard-to-find items. All-inclusive catalog available for $1, refundable with first order.*)

Zweigart®, Somerset, New Jersey (*all Mono deluxe "orange-line" canvas, #10, #12, #14, #18, Congress cloth #24 mesh, waste canvas #14 mesh, Interlock canvas, and Quick Point canvas*)

INTRODUCTION

It has been said that the language of the needle is universal and that regardless of age, education, or cultural background, the lovers of stitching are bound together by a magical thread.

Needlepoint is one of the most popular forms of needlework. It is so easy to master that beginners can achieve excellent results on the first attempt. I have taught the basic tent stitch to seven-year-old Girl Scout Brownies and octogenarians at a nursing home.

It will also offer many interesting techniques and challenges to the advanced canvas worker who can produce creative and imaginative works of art.

The equipment required to get started is simple and inexpensive. Some canvas, yarn, a blunt-tip needle, a pair of scissors, and one stitch are all you need.

This book will serve as a working text with step-by-step diagrams and a photograph for each stitch. It will be the complete stitch reference guide for everyone who works needlepoint and canvas embroidery. I have used the most popular name for each stitch but included all alternative names that I could find. New stitches are constantly being developed, some by accident, some adapted from other needlecrafts, and some by design. It is, therefore, impossible to include every stitch in existence that can be used for canvas work. I am sure you will find that most of the known stitches from all over the world have been included.

There is a chapter describing the tools and accessories that are used, with photographs of each item for easy identification.

I have also included an explanation of the vocabulary peculiar to needlepoint and canvas embroidery and detailed instructions for the *basics*, including descriptions and photographs of the different types of canvas, needles, yarns, and other fibers. You will learn how to calculate yarn yardage, choose stitches, work a design from a drawing or graph, and to block, mount, and finish the completed needlework with a minimum of expense or expertise.

A chapter has been included to explain the special techniques used with plastic canvas.

Always remember, this is *your* needlepoint and canvas stitch dictionary from A to Z.

The Basics

TOOLS AND ACCESSORIES

You do not need many tools to work needlepoint and canvas stitches. In fact, you can get started with canvas, yarn, and a needle.

I must admit, however, that I love to use many of the tools and accessories that enhance the working and make it easier to master.

BLOCKING FRAME AND SOLUTION

Marie's blocking frame (**Easy Blocker**) and **Spray 'N Block®** solution are wonderful products that reduce blocking time for a piece of needlepoint to about 60 minutes.

CANVAS

Four types of Zweigart® canvas were used for this book. (See "Canvas," page 8.)

Mono Canvas

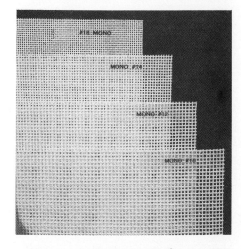

Interlock Mono

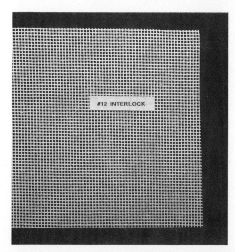

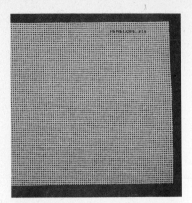

Penelope #14 (2-thread)

Quick Point #5

Congress Cloth

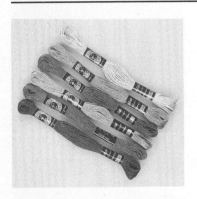

FLOSS

Many stitchers have chosen to work on a finer canvas such as Congress cloth or silk gauze. Six-strand embroidery floss is used more often than any other type of thread on these finer canvases. I have chosen to use **Anchor**® floss for the samples in this book for the sheen, wearability, and large selection of colors.

FRAY CHECK®

This is a colorless plastic liquid solution that locks fabric, yarn, or threads to prevent fraying. It was used on many samples in this book. (See "Materials and Supplies," page viii.)

GLOVES

Handeze® therapeutic craft gloves, shown in the photo, are stretch Lycra gloves that are said to reduce hand stress from fatigue, arthritis, carpal tunnel syndrome, and much more. They're brand-new and worth a try. (See "Materials and Supplies," page viii.)

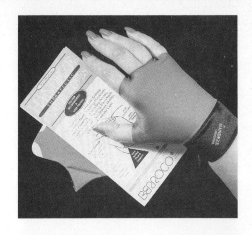

MAGNETIC BOARD

This is a very useful aid for the stitcher who follows written instructions or works with charts and stitch diagrams. They are available in many sizes. The **Lo-Ran®** boards are shown here. I recommend their accessory magnetic line magnifier for easy reading.

NEEDLES

All canvas stitchery is worked with a blunt-tip tapestry needle. They are available in sizes #13 to #26. (See "Measurements," page 14) **Susan Bates®** tapestry needles were used to make the samples in this book.

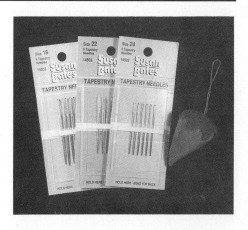

Tapestry needles are also available in 24K-gold–plated and platinum-plated for extra-smooth stitching. Try them—it's fun to be a little extravagant.

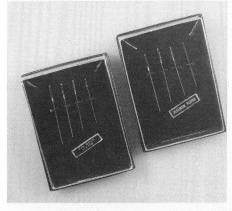

PLASTIC CANVAS

Plastic canvas has become so popular that it is now available in almost every shape and size imaginable. (See "Plastic Canvas," page 9.)

PERLE COTTON

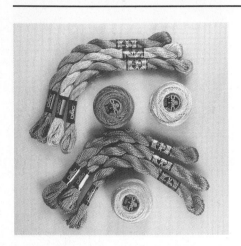

This twisted 2-ply thread is available in three sizes, #3, #5, and #8, and in a large range of colors.

SCISSORS

4" thread clip

To work on canvas it is necessary to have at least two pairs of scissors: a large pair for cutting the canvas and a small pair with a sharp point for cutting the yarn or thread.

The gingher® line of scissors is considered by many to be the premier line of scissors available. They were used for the preparation of the samples in this book. (See "Materials and Supplies," page viii.) *Never cut paper or plastic with scissors used to cut thread or fabric.*

The following are my favorite scissors for needle-work.

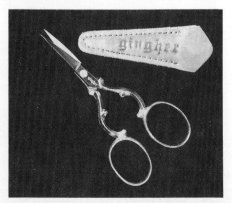

3½" embroidery scissors

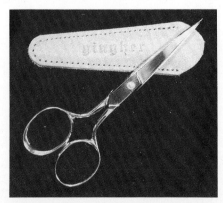

4" embroidery scissors

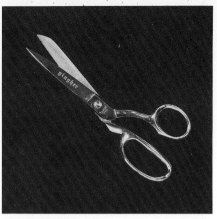

8″ bent trimmers

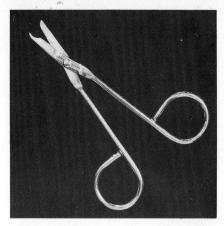

suture scissors

SCROLL FRAME

A scroll frame consists of two sidebars and two horizontal rods or heavy dowels with web fabric attached. It is put together and secured with bolts and wing nuts. The canvas is sewn or pinned to the web fabric and rolled over the rods until it is taut. It is usually used for large-scale needlework.

SEAM AND STITCH RIPPER

This little tool is a must for removing your mistakes quickly and safely.

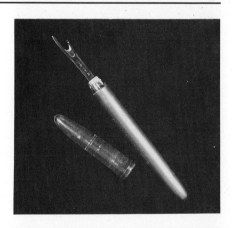

SHARPENING STONE

A fine-grit whetstone is used to sharpen and hone the blades of knife-edge scissors and shears. Occasional honing will keep your fine scissors sharp for years.

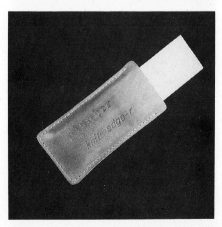

SILK GAUZE

This is a fabric used for petit point, miniatures, and appliqué (faces and hands, for example).

SILTEX®

This is a lightweight polyester ground fabric that is available in #18 mesh.

STANDS

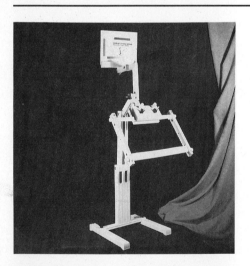

Many needlepoint stitches require the use of both hands (stab method), so a good floor stand is essential to hold your stretcher strips or other frames.

The stand in the photo, called a **Rocky Giraffe,** is a wonderful all-around utility stand that is made of rock maple, is adjustable, and collapses for travel to courses, meetings, and seminars.

STRETCHER STRIPS

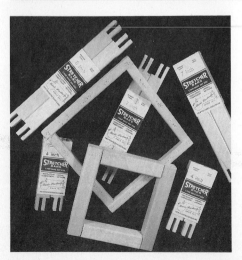

I recommend the use of stretcher strips for most needlepoint projects. They are made in sizes from 4" up. (See "Materials and Supplies," page viii.) The canvas is attached with thumbtacks, making it possible to exert an even tension both horizontally and vertically.

THREADERS

This little tool is a necessity for the times when "tired" or "mature" eyes need help to thread the needle. The **LoRan® threader** shown here is also available as part of a needlework accessory kit and includes a magnetic needle case and a magnetic needle holder that can be attached to the canvas.

WORK LIGHT

It is important to have good lighting when you do needlework. Always place the light source over the shoulder *opposite* the working hand. Therefore, if you are right-handed, the light should come over your left shoulder; if you are left-handed, the light should come over your right shoulder.

YARNS

The stitch samples in this book were worked using the two major types of yarn for needlepoint: tapestry and Persian.

Tapestry Yarn

Laine Tapisserie (tapestry yarn) by **Anchor®** was used for stitch samples in this book. (See "Wool Yarns," page 11.)

Persian Yarn

DMC® Floralia® (Persian yarn) was used for stitch samples in this book. (See "Wool Yarns," page 11.)

METALLIC THREADS

The **Kreinik** metallic threads used in this book are available in blending filament, #8 fine braid, #16 medium braid, #32 heavy braid, and 1/16" ribbon. They all produce wonderful accent effects.

RIBBON THREADS

These 1/8" and 1/4" ribbons are an example of the unusual appearance you can achieve using an unusual fiber. It is exceptional for bargello work.

CANVAS

Canvas is a heavily sized fabric that is available in 100 percent cotton, polyester, linen, plastic, and silk gauze in a wide range of sizes or threads per inch.

Each type of canvas has a use for a different needlepoint project.

There are three basic types of canvas: Mono or evenweave (single-thread canvas), Interlock (2 fine threads crossed by 1 heavier thread), and Penelope (double-thread canvas).

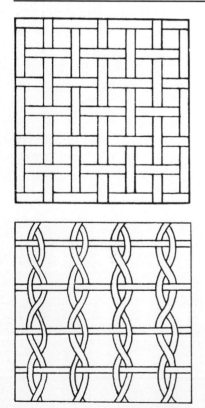

Mono Canvas

This is an evenweave canvas formed of single woven horizontal and vertical canvas threads. It is available in #10, #12, #13, #14, #16, #18, #20, and #24 threads to the inch. The #24 mesh to the inch is called Congress cloth and is available in many colors. (See "Tools and Accessories," page 1.)

Interlock Mono Canvas

Interlock Mono canvas closely resembles evenweave Mono canvas. It is very different in construction, with 2 vertical canvas threads woven with a single horizontal canvas thread.

Sometimes the threads are bonded together at each intersection of vertical and horizontal threads. Interlock canvas will not ravel and can be trimmed close to the finished work.

This canvas is available in #4, #5, #6, #7, #10, #12, #13, #14, and #18 threads to the inch, or mesh.

Interlock Mono does not distort as easily as regular Mono canvas, but is not recommended for any work that needs "give," such as a chair cushion or any upholstery.

Penelope Canvas

Penelope canvas (also called double-thread canvas) is constructed of woven pairs of vertical canvas threads that are crossed and woven with pairs of horizontal canvas threads.

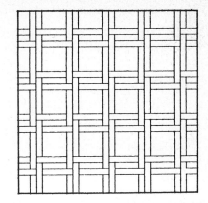

Both large stitches and small petit point stitches can be worked on the same Penelope canvas. For large stitches, the pairs of threads are treated and worked as 1 thread; for petit point the pairs of threads are separated into a regular Mono evenweave and stitched singly. This canvas is an ideal choice where detail is required in some areas and a larger stitch in others.

Penelope canvas is also available in #3.5, #5, and #7 threads to the inch and is called rug canvas.

Waste Canvas

Waste canvas is another double-thread canvas. It is very lightweight and is not intended for use as a ground fabric.

It is used as a temporary surface that is attached to fabric unsuitable for embroidering so that the stitches can be worked through both the canvas and the fabric. Then the canvas is moistened to soften the sizing and the individual canvas threads are removed one at a time, leaving the embroidered stitches on the base fabric.

SILK GAUZE

Silk gauze is an interlocked Mono-weave fabric used for canvas stitches, fine petit point, and miniatures.

It is very lightweight and is available in #24, #30, #34, #40, #48, #54, #60, #72, and #87 threads to the inch.

Siltex® is a lightweight polyester fabric that is constructed in the same manner as silk gauze. It is available in mesh size #18.

PLASTIC CANVAS

Plastic canvas is generally used to make boxes, tissue box covers, toys, and other small craft projects.

It comes in sheets approximately 10½" × 13½" (27 × 34 cm) in #7, #10, and #14 threads to the inch; in circles, diamonds, and hexagons in a number of varying sizes; and by the yard in a lighter weight. The yard goods are more flexible than the sheets.

Plastic canvas is excellent for teaching beginners, children, and elderly people. (See "Plastic Canvas," below.)

PLASTIC CANVAS

Plastic canvas is used by craftspeople, needleworkers, children, beginners, and the elderly. It is made of nonwoven molded plastic with holes and simulated threads and comes in many shapes and sizes.

The most common mesh sizes are 7, 10, and 14 threads to the inch, with #7 mesh plastic canvas most often used for craft projects. It is sold in 10⅝" × 13⅝" and 13⅝" × 21⅝" sheets; 3" and 4" squares; 3"-, 4"-, 6"-, and 9"-diameter circles; diamond shapes; by the yard; and in many specialty shapes such as alphabet letters, numbers, hearts, and ovals.

Plastic canvas is manufactured in different weights ranging from very firm and rigid to soft and pliable. It is usually made in a clear plastic but is also available in white and a variety of colors.

Specialty shapes and sizes are easily cut with a crafts knife or heavy-duty scissors.

YARNS FOR PLASTIC CANVAS

The yarn or fiber selected for use on plastic canvas is usually determined by the intended use of the project. For example, if the project will be handled frequently I would suggest a washable acrylic worsted weight yarn. Almost any yarn or fiber can be used on plastic canvas.

Worsted-Weight Yarn

This is the most popular and commonly used yarn for plastic canvas because of availability, color selection, and cost. One strand of worsted yarn has 4 plies and covers the canvas very well.

It is made in a variety of fibers, extending the versatility and usage.

Sport-Weight Yarn

Sport yarn has the same advantages as worsted with regard to fiber content, color selection, and cost; but since it is lighter in weight, it must be doubled to cover a #7 mesh canvas, thereby increasing the project cost.

Tapestry Yarn

This yarn is a lightweight wool yarn that works well on #10 mesh but requires doubling for #7 mesh.

It is available in a wide variety of colors and shades of a color. That makes it desirable for color blending. It is more expensive than worsted yarn.

Persian Yarn

Persian yarn, like tapestry yarn, is made of wool and comes in a wide variety of colors and shades of a color. It is made of 3 plies that can be separated and used as 1 or 2 ply or even 3–6 plies as required. This is also a more expensive yarn than worsted.

Perle Cotton

Number 3 perle cotton is used to give the work a sheen or lacelike look. It will cover on #10 mesh canvas.

Embroidery Floss

Embroidery floss is used for a detailed area or an accent. It can be used in multiple plies on #10 mesh canvas. (See "Plastic Canvas Yarn and Needle Chart," below.)

NEEDLES FOR PLASTIC CANVAS

All stitching on plastic canvas is done with a blunt-tip tapestry needle. (See "Tools and Accessories," page 1.) The needle size is determined by the plastic canvas mesh size and the thickness of the yarn. See "Plastic Canvas Yarn and Needle Chart," below.

PLASTIC CANVAS YARN AND NEEDLE CHART		
Yarn	7 Mesh	10 Mesh
Worsted-Weight Yarn	1–2 strands	NO
Sport-Weight Yarn	2–3 strands	1 strand
Tapestry Yarn	2–3 strands	1 strand
Persian Yarn	1–2 strands	2–3 plies
#3 Perle Cotton	1–2 strands	1 strand
Embroidery Floss	12 plies	6 plies
Needles	#18 Tapestry	#20 Tapestry

CUTTING PLASTIC CANVAS

Plastic canvas can be cut to size or shape with scissors or a crafts knife.

Most instructions will give a thread count somewhere near the chart. This count will tell you the number of threads in the height and width of the canvas. *It does not mean the holes.*

Always cut as close to the thread as possible to avoid creating "nubs" that will snag the yarn and protrude from the finished work. It is best that all pieces in a project be cut at the same time.

JOINING AND EDGING PIECES

The Overcast Stitch or the Binding Stitch is used to cover the edges of the canvas or to join canvas pieces.

Overcast Stitch

The sample is worked on #7 mesh plastic canvas.

It may be necessary to stitch through the same hole twice for complete coverage.

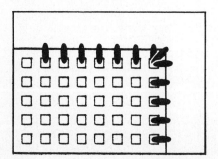

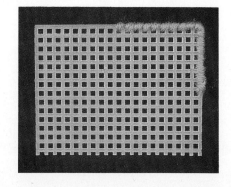

Binding Stitch

(Braided cross-stitch)

The sample is worked on #7 mesh plastic canvas.

This stitch covers the edges of the plastic canvas with a full braided edging.

Following the diagrams, start at the left-hand corner edge, coming to the front at **1**. Go over the top at **2**, over the top again, and back down into the starting hole at **3**.

Bring the yarn over the top into **4** and back over at **5**.

Repeat across the edge, forming the braid as shown in the next diagram.

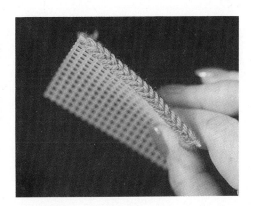

CLEANING AND WASHING

Do not dry-clean any plastic canvas work. The chemicals used in the process could distort or even dissolve plastic.

Plastic canvas can be hand-washed in warm water with a very mild detergent if acrylic yarn is used for the stitching. Squeeze gently—do not rub the stitches. If pills form on the yarn, snip them carefully with a scissors.

Plastic canvas can melt in the dryer; *air-dry only.*

YARNS AND THREADS

Any type of yarn can be used for canvas stitches when the piece is meant for decorative purposes.

If the project is to be used for upholstery fabric, cushions, rugs, or any object that will be subject to wear, use only fibers designed for use on canvas.

The following are examples of some of the most popular threads and yarns available for canvas work.

WOOL YARNS

Tapestry Yarn

Tapestry yarn is composed of 4 pieces that are used in a single strand (not separated). It works best on diagonal stitches.

Tapestry yarn is manufactured in a large range of colors (for example, **Laine Tapisserie** by **Anchor**® comes in 430 colors) and works well on #10 or #12 mesh canvas. It was used for many samples in this book.

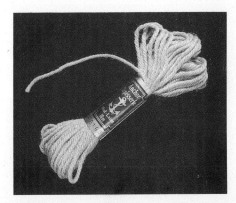

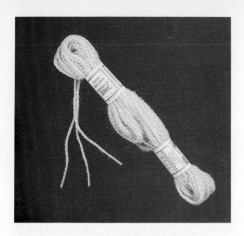

Persian Yarn

This is the most popular type of yarn for all canvas stitches. Each strand is composed of three 2-ply strands that can easily be separated and used in single or multiple strands that will match all canvas mesh sizes. **DMC® Floralia®** was used for many samples in this book. It is readily available and comes in a wide range of colors.

COTTON THREADS

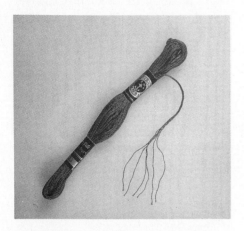

Cotton Floss

Six-strand cotton floss has become a very popular choice for canvas work in recent years. It comes in a large range of colors. It is easily separated or combined to form any weight thread desired. **Susan Bates® Anchor®** floss was used to work many samples in this book.

Perle Cotton

This is a twisted 2-ply thread that is available in three sizes or weights: #3, #5, and #8. The individual strands *cannot* be separated, but within any one weight they can be combined into any number of strands for use on most canvas sizes. You may see this thread referred to as perle cotton (English) or *coton perlé* (French).

Flower Thread

This is a soft matte-finish cotton thread that is available in 180 colors and can be combined for use on canvas.

MEDICIS®

Medicis® is a fine crewel-type smooth yarn used for needlepoint. It is made in a single ply that is meant to be combined for use on any size canvas. It is smoother than Persian wool. **Medicis®** by **DMC®** is available in 150 colors.

SILK THREADS

Stranded silk floss gives the canvas work an elegant lustrous appearance. It can easily be separated into individual strands and recombined for use in any size canvas. I recommend 7-ply Soie d'Alger by **Au Ver a Soie**®. It is made in about 400 colors.

SYNTHETIC THREADS AND YARNS

There are a large variety of synthetic metallic and rayon viscose threads available for use on canvas. Most are difficult to handle and should be used only by expert stitchers.

The ⅛" and ¼" ribbons used in the bargello chapter (page 16) are good examples of the original look you can achieve with common stitches using ribbon.

Acrylic yarns are a good choice for use on plastic canvas. They are made in a wide variety of colors and weights and can easily be washed. (See "Plastic Canvas," page 9.)

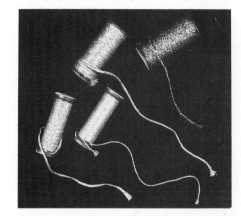

The Kreinik metallic threads are made of aluminized polyester films that are processed to make yarns suitable for needlework. They are washable, drycleanable, nontarnishing, and reasonably priced. The effect is spectacular when they are used for an accent stitch.

For needlepoint stitching, I recommend you try #8 fine braid, #16 medium braid, #32 heavy braid, and ¹⁄₁₆" ribbon. The blending filament gives an attractive sparkle when added to other yarns and threads for stitching.

GRAIN OF YARN

All spun yarn or thread has a grain. If you work against the grain, the yarn will become worn and fuzzy.

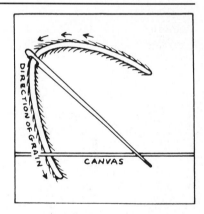

To determine the direction of the grain, gently rub the strand between your thumb and index finger. In one direction the fibers will feel smooth; in the other the fibers will feel fuzzy and rough. Practice with different yarns and threads.

The needle is always threaded so that the thread can be pulled through the canvas with the fibers pointing away from the canvas (in the smooth direction).

NEEDLES

A tapestry needle is used for canvas stitchery. It has a blunt tip and an elongated eye. This type of needle is made in sizes #13 to #26, ranging from large (#13) to fine (#26).

Always use the correct size needle for the yarn and canvas. A needle that is too large will distort the canvas threads and cause uneven stitches, not to mention sore fingers from pulling hard on the needle. A needle that is too small will pinch the yarn and cause it to wear quickly and shred. Keep your needles clean by using an emery-filled "strawberry." See the "Canvas, Needle, Yarn Length Chart" below.

CANVAS, NEEDLE, YARN LENGTH CHART		
Canvas Mesh	Needle Size	Yarn Length
#10	#18	24"–30"
#12	#18 or #20	24"–30"
#14	#20 or #22	16"–24"
#16	#22	16"–24"
#18	#24	16"
Congress cloth	#26	16"
#30 Silk gauze	#26	16"
#40 Silk gauze	#26 or Crewel	16"

MEASUREMENTS

A basic knowledge of measurements and conversions is needed by all needleworkers.

The question most often asked is how to determine the size of a design when a given pattern chart is to be worked on one size canvas instead of another. The formula for making this determination is simple and requires only the most basic mathematical ability.

Always start by counting the number of squares on the chart (squares = stitches) in both the horizontal and vertical directions.

Next count the number of horizontal and vertical threads in one square inch on your canvas (if you don't already know the canvas size).

The formula is: *Design area divided by threads per inch equals size of finished piece.* Therefore, a 30 × 30-stitch design worked on #14 canvas would read: 30 ÷ 14 = 2.1".

That is the working or finished design area. *Always* add 3" on *each* of the four sides as a work border before you cut the canvas.

VOCABULARY

Every needle craft has a special vocabulary or language. It is necessary to familiarize yourself with these words and phrases *before* attempting to read any directions.

A.N.G. American Needlework Guild

accent stitch A surface stitch used for color or texture.

appliqué Attaching a worked canvas to another canvas that is usually of a different size or mesh.

away knot This is a starting knot used when there is no stitching that can hide the beginning thread. It is usually placed about 3"–4" away from the first stitch, cut when the stitching is complete, and woven through the back of the stitches.

awl A sharp-pointed tool that is used for enlarging a canvas hole.

bargello Florentine embroidery (see page 16).

border stitch This is a wide stitch that is always worked in a straight line (horizontal or vertical).

canvas This is the ground fabric for needlepoint. It has a grid structure made of equally spaced horizontal and vertical canvas threads.

centering To find the center of a canvas, fold the canvas in half lengthwise, then in half crosswise. Make a mark where the two folds bisect each other.

clean hole This is an empty or unworked canvas hole. Always bring the needle up from the back in a clean hole.

compensation stitch The *partial stitch* needed to make a straight edge or complete an area.

composite stitch A stitch made up of two or more stitches.

Congress cloth A fine canvas (24 threads to the inch) that is made in many colors.

crewel yarn This is a very thin 2-ply yarn that can be used for needlepoint on a fine mesh canvas.

dandruff Flecks of canvas that show between the stitches. Usually the yarn is not heavy enough or the stitch tension is too tight.

dirty hole An occupied hole (one that has a stitch). Always work from a clean hole into a dirty hole.

ditch This is a channel formed between 2 stitches or 2 canvas threads.

dry cleaning Necessary for cleaning all wool and silk fibers. *Do not wash these fibers.*

E.G.A. Embroiderers' Guild of America

emery A powder filling in a strawberry-shaped cotton form used to clean and sharpen needles.

encroaching stitches These are stitches that overlap one row of stitching with the previous row.

eye The hole in the top of the needle, which holds the thread.

eyelet stitch A stitch that is worked *into* a central hole.

fences These are nubs on plastic canvas that poke through the stitches on poorly trimmed canvas.

filling stitch A stitch used to fill a predetermined shape on a ground fabric.

floss Six-stranded cotton embroidery thread.

frame Usually wooden stretcher bars or strips used to keep the canvas taut during stitching to prevent stitch distortion.

garage A thick stitch such as Scotch or Rhodes placed in the border area of the canvas and used to "park" needles.

gauge This is the count of horizontal and vertical threads in 1 square inch of canvas. If you have 10 threads per inch, the canvas is called #10, #10 mesh, or 10-gauge.

gros point Any needlework on a large mesh canvas, usually #10 or larger.

grounding stitch Any stitch that can be used to cover large areas or background.

guest thread This is the thread going down in an occupied hole. See host thread.

half drop This refers to the arrangement of

stitches where the top of the second stitch starts at the center of the first stitch, forming a stepped appearance.

hoop This is a round frame used to hold fabric taut while stitching. *Never use a hoop on canvas.*

host thread This is the thread in an occupied hole. See guest thread.

islands Single stitches.

isolated stitch A stitch worked individually, usually as a surface motif.

journey A trip across the row. Some stitches require two or more journeys to complete the stitch.

laid work This is a stitching technique in which long threads are laid across a shape. The stitch is worked *over* these threads.

laying tool A stroking needle used to align the threads so they will lay flat. You can use a needle trolley, Teko Bari, or even a long rug needle.

length of thread Do not use a thread or yarn that is longer than needed (usually 16"–24"). Long lengths will usually wear thin or even shred. (See the "Canvas, Needle, Yarn Length Chart," page 13.)

mesh The place where the horizontal and vertical canvas threads cross.

Mono canvas This is an evenweave canvas formed by single horizontal and vertical threads. (See "Canvas," page 8.)

motif stitch A surface stitch that is worked individually, an accent stitch.

needlepoint A generic term for canvas stitches.

needles Needles come in various sizes (see "Needles," page 13). When you are unsure of the correct size needle to use for a particular canvas, just put one down into a canvas hole. If it drops through, it's okay to use.

needle threader This is a small metal disk or rectangle with a hook to catch the yarn or thread after you easily slip the yarn or thread through the eye of the needle.

nubs Small balls of yarn on the surface of needlework caused by wear or rubbing. *Also see* fences.

open stitch A stitch that lets the ground fabric (canvas) show.

orts These are the small pieces of yarn or thread that are trimmed from the starting and ending threads.

ort bag Used to collect your orts. Some people save them to use as stuffing.

Penelope canvas A canvas formed by woven pairs of horizontal and vertical canvas threads. Also called 2-thread canvas. (See "Canvas," page 8.)

pens Always test to be sure the pen or marker you choose is waterproof. *Never use a ballpoint pen on canvas.*

perle cotton This is a twisted 2-ply thread.

Persian yarn This is a 3-ply (three 2-ply strands) yarn that can be separated into individual strands. (See "Yarns and Threads," page 11.)

petit point Needlepoint that is worked on a fine mesh canvas or silk gauze.

plastic bags Do not store yarn, threads, or canvas in *sealed* plastic bags. Moisture can form inside the bag, causing the fiber materials to mat or even rot.

primary hole The hole or space between the canvas threads where the needle comes up from the back to the front.

quick point Any needlepoint on canvas larger than #10, usually rug canvas.

right side The side of the needlework meant to be seen.

ripping Sooner or later you'll have to rip out an error in your stitching. Be methodical and careful to avoid cutting the canvas threads. I like using suture scissors (with a hook on one blade). The British call this "unpicking," but I prefer an alternative and gentler term, "retrostitching."

selvage This is the woven edge of the canvas. It is *always* held at the side of the work.

sewing or swing method Stitching on canvas *without* a frame. The needle is inserted in a canvas hole and back up under 1 or more threads in the same motion. Then the yarn is pulled completely through to the front, completing the stitch.

shot or sand bags These are small cotton bags filled with lead shot or sand and used as weights to hold down stretcher strip frames for stitching at a table.

stab method The canvas is held taut on a frame. The stitch is worked in two motions. The needle is stabbed through a canvas hole from the back and the yarn is pulled completely through to the front. Then the needle is stabbed down into the next hole and the yarn is pulled completely to the back.

straight stitches Upright stitches worked over horizontal canvas threads.

stranded cotton This is the British name for floss.

stripping Separating the 3 plies of Persian yarn or the 6 strands of floss into individual threads.

tapestry needle A blunt-tip, large-eye needle used for needlepoint.

tapestry yarn This is a twisted 4-ply yarn used mainly for needlepoint.

twisted thread This is caused by rolling the needle as you stitch. When this occurs, let the yarn and needle dangle. The thread will unwind by itself.

warp The canvas threads that run lengthwise (from the loom).

waste knot This is the only acceptable knot used in needlework. It is used to hold the yarn or thread in place *temporarily* so that it can be covered with stitches. Cut it off as soon as possible.

weft The canvas threads that run horizontally and are woven with the warp threads.

woof This is the Old English word for *weft.*

wrong side This is the side of the needlepoint that is not seen, or the back of the canvas, where the threads are started and ended.

yarn Any fiber that is stranded. It can be made of wool, cotton, silk, acrylic, nylon, etc.

BARGELLO

Basically, bargello is an old form of embroidery known by many names in various part of the world. It has been referred to as Florentine embroidery, Flame stitch, Point de Hongrie, or Hungarian stitching.

The patterns are based on repeated geometric designs worked with long vertical or upright Gobelin stitches using 2–6 horizontal canvas threads and color to create optical illusions.

Bargello patterns can use other stitches, but usually they consist of multiple upright Gobelin stitches that are worked in steps around the canvas forming rows.

These steps are usually worked in a 4-2 pattern (over 4 horizontal and 2 vertical canvas threads) that forms steep peaks and valleys. A flatter pattern is achieved by working a 4-1 pattern (over 4 horizontal and 1 vertical canvas threads).

Bargello stitches *must* be worked with a loose, even tension to cover the canvas threads evenly and completely.

Always work *from* an unoccupied canvas hole *into* an occupied canvas hole.

The following bargello designs were chosen to show a selection of patterns, from easy to difficult. The illustrations provide only a tiny taste of this fascinating form of embroidery. More information and more complicated patterns can be found in books devoted solely to bargello embroidery.

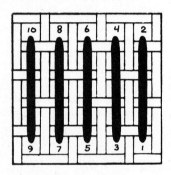

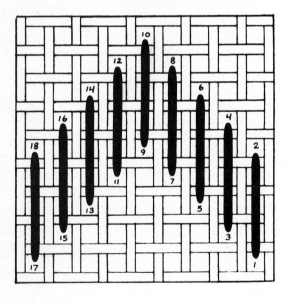

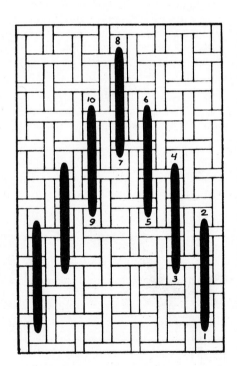

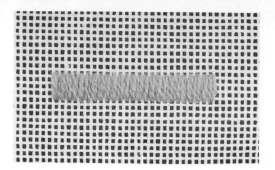
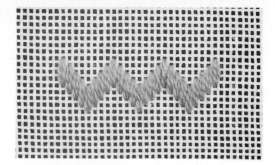
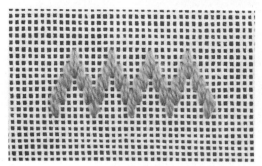

BARGELLO PATTERN #1
(scallop, wave)

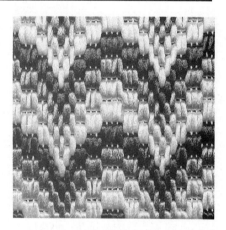

The sample is worked on #12 Zweigart® Mono canvas using ⅛″ ribbon.

This is a good example of a line pattern. It is an easy 4-2 wave or scallop shape. Notice that using 4 shades of 1 color defines the shape.

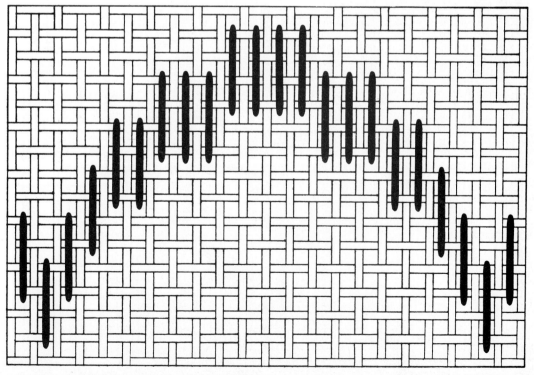

BARGELLO PATTERN #2
(pomegranate)

The sample is worked on Zweigart® Congress cloth using Anchor® floss in 4 shades of blue.

This is another easy pattern. The individual motifs share a common outline (black symbol on diagram).

There are many variations possible with this pattern. (See Bargello Pattern #3.)

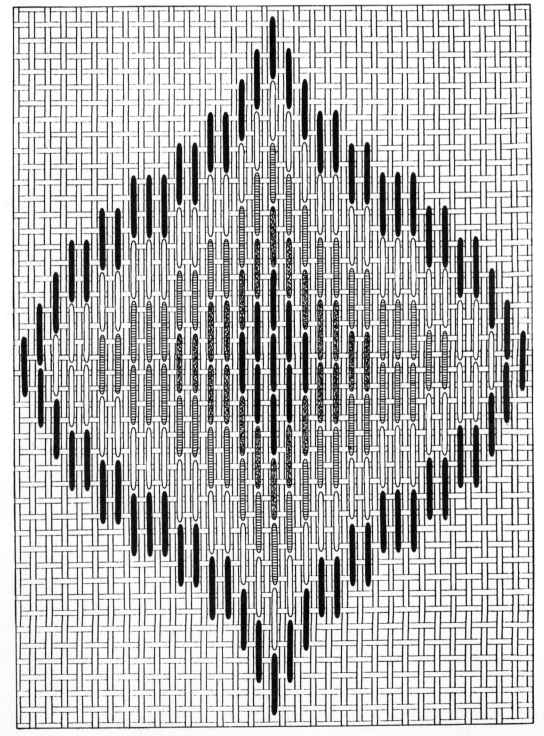

BARGELLO PATTERN #3
(pomegranate variation)

The sample is worked on Zweigart® Congress cloth using Anchor® floss in 4 shades of gray and 3 shades of blue.

This is a variation of Bargello Pattern #2 (pomegranate). Notice the wavelike optical illusion formed.

Another variation can be made by reversing the shades (the lightest shade is replaced by the darkest and the darkest is replaced by the lightest shade. The middle shades are also reversed.)

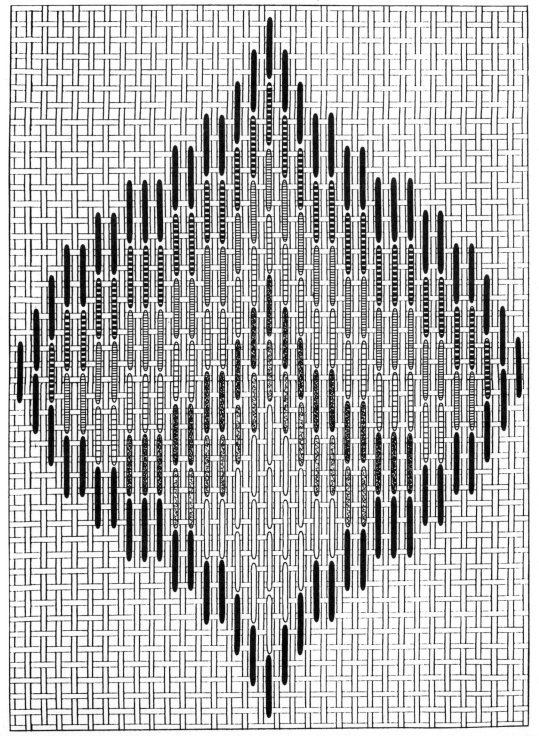

BARGELLO PATTERN #4
(argyle)

The sample is worked on Zweigart® Congress cloth using Anchor® floss in 3 shades of blue and 1 purple.

This is a more complicated 4-2 pattern that takes a simple diamond shape and forms an overall argyle pattern using a common outline (black symbol on diagram).

Notice that the lines change direction to make the diamond shape.

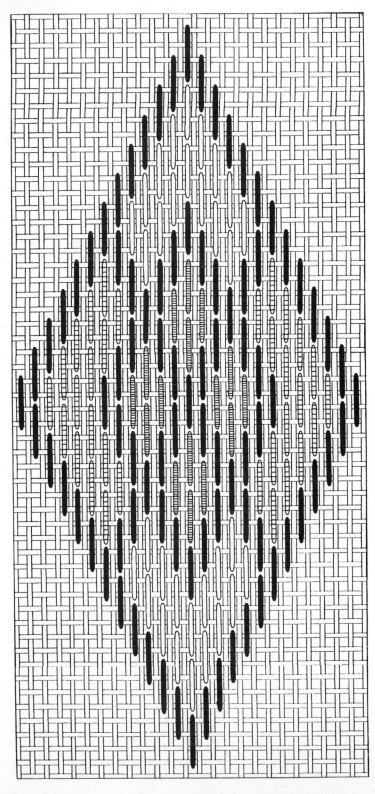

BARGELLO PATTERN #5
(woven, woven ribbons)

The sample is worked on Zweigart® Congress cloth using Anchor® floss in 4 shades of blue, 4 shades of gray, and 1 purple.

This is a difficult 4-2 step pattern that gives a woven illusion to the pattern. The ribbons can be worked in 4 shades of any 2 colors; however, always use another dark color for the separating small diamond shapes.

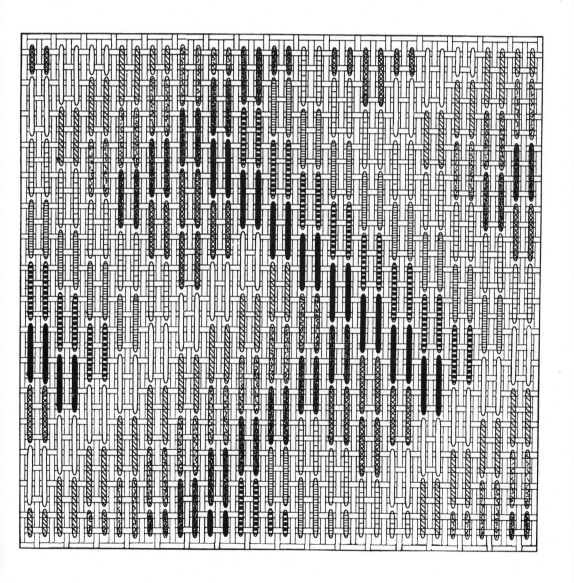

BARGELLO PATTERN #6
(trees, lollipops)

The sample is worked on #10 Zweigart® Mono canvas using black, white, gray, and 2 shades of brown ¼″ ribbon.

In this pattern, the treelike shapes are worked individually.

Although any yarn can be used to create this pattern, I have chosen to use ribbon to show how an unconventional fiber can be used to create an unusual texture and give a totally different look to the bargello pattern.

Note: See color photographs.

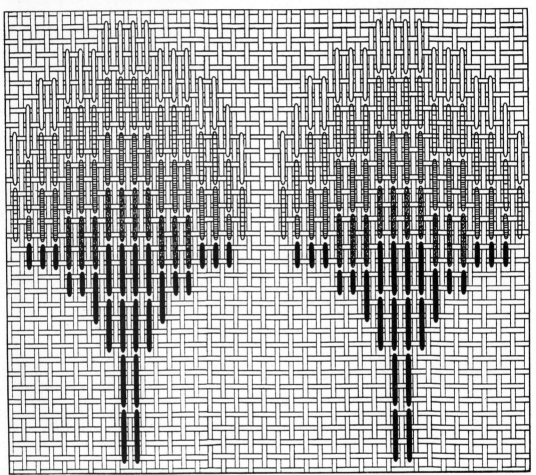

BARGELLO PATTERNS

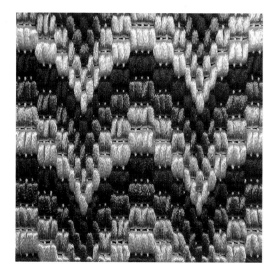

Bargello Pattern #1 (scallop, wave)

Bargello Pattern #2 (pomegranate)

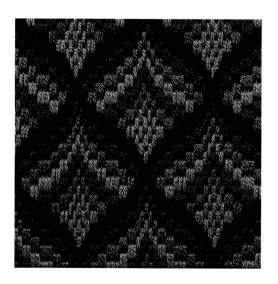

Bargello Pattern #3 (pomegranate variation)

Bargello Pattern #4 (argyle)

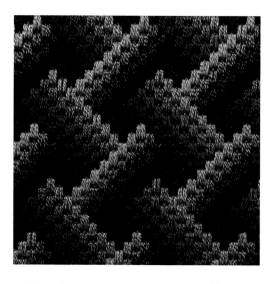

Bargello Pattern #5 (woven, woven ribbons)

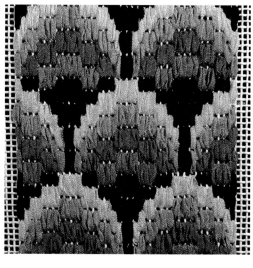

Bargello Pattern #6 (trees, lollipops)

PROJECTS

Belt

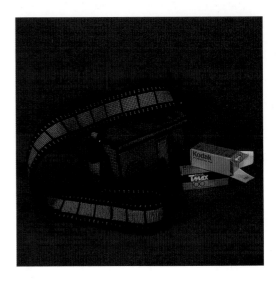

Camera Case with Strap

Dale's Stitching Lady

Eyeglass Case

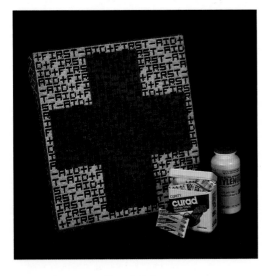

First Aid Box

Flask Cover

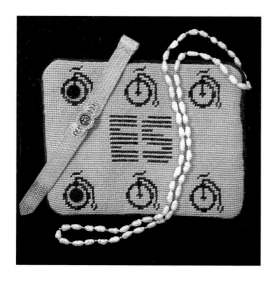

Jewelry Case/Tool Case

Key Chains

Luggage Rack

Picture of George

Pocket

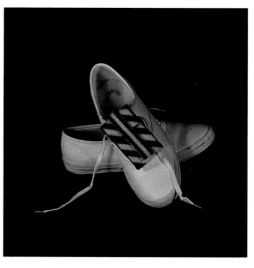

Sneaker Key/Coin Holder

Soda/Beer Can Covers

Squash Racquet Case

Tennis Racquet Cover

Tennis Equipment Wall Rack

Tissue Box Cover

Visor

STITCH PATTERNS

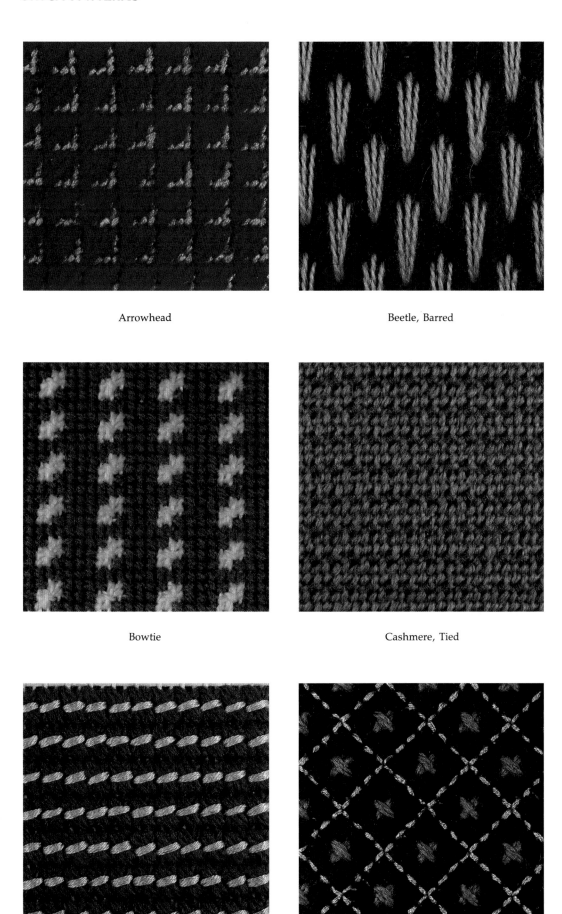

Arrowhead

Beetle, Barred

Bowtie

Cashmere, Tied

Cross, Hitched

Crossed Diamond

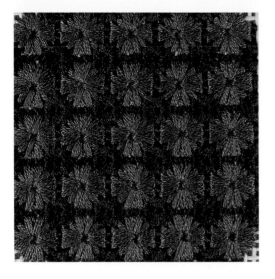

Daisies, Squared

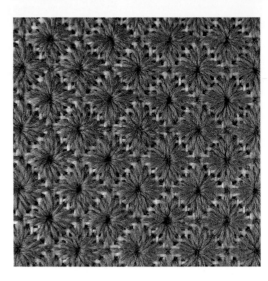

Diamond Eye

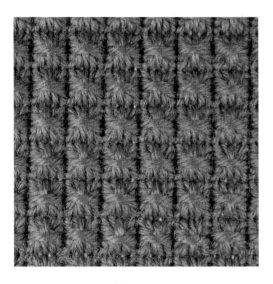

Double Leviathan

Eyelet, Six-Sided

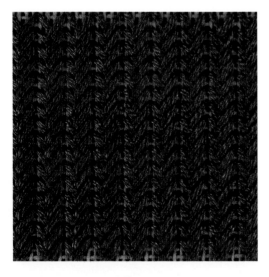

Fern

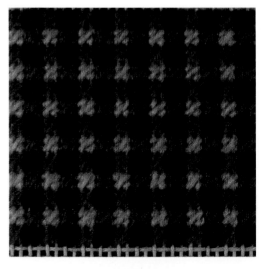

Gingham Mosaic

Herringbone

Hilton Amadeus

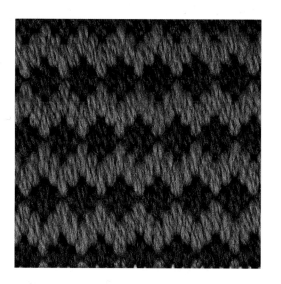

Hungarian, Grounding 2

Leaf 1

Leaf, Medallion

Oriental

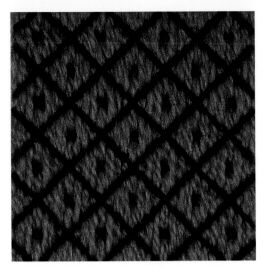

Pavilion, Tied with Backstitch

Rhodes, Octagonal
(with Rhodes, Diamond)

Scotch II, Alternating

Star, Slanting

Triple Twist

Woven Ribbons

The Stitch Dictionary
"A to Z"

A

ALGERIAN EYE
(star)

The sample is worked on #10 Zweigart® Mono canvas with DMC® Floralia® (3-ply Persian yarn).

The Algerian Eye stitch consists of 8 stitches, each worked over 2 canvas threads in a clockwise direction with each stitch coming from the outside and entering the center hole to form an eyelet. The harder you pull on each stitch, the larger the eyelet becomes.

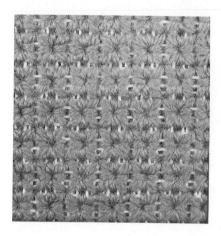

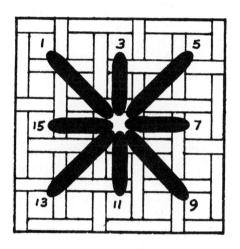

ALGERIAN EYE, DOUBLE
(double eye)

The sample is worked on #12 Zweigart® Mono canvas with DMC® Floralia® (3-ply Persian yarn).

This is a variation of the Algerian Eye stitch. Each of the 8 legs of the stitch is worked *twice*, resulting in 16 stitches going into the center hole.

Try to lay the pairs of thread or yarn next to each other neatly for a smooth effect.

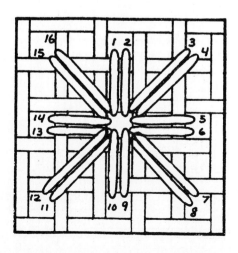

ALGERIAN EYE, ELONGATED

The sample is worked on #14 Zweigart® Mono canvas with DMC® Floralia® (3-ply Persian yarn).

This variation of the Algerian Eye stitch is worked over 4 horizontal and 2 vertical canvas threads.

All the stitches are worked *into* 1 central hole. Follow the numbering on the diagram exactly as shown.

This stitch is worked in 1 color.

ALGERIAN FILLING

The sample is worked on #10 Zweigart® Mono canvas with DMC® Floralia® (3-ply Persian yarn).

This stitch is made of blocks of 3 vertical straight stitches worked over 4 horizontal canvas threads in a stepped pattern.

Work the first block (**1-2, 3-4, 5-6**), then work the second block, starting 2 horizontal canvas threads below (**7-8, 9-10, 11-12**). Continue in this manner. Compensating stitches have been added in the diagram.

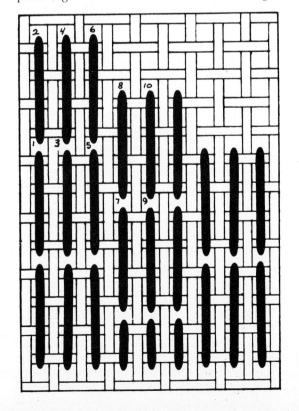

ALICIA LACE
(four-way continental)

The sample is worked on #14 Zweigart® Mono canvas with DMC® #5 perle cotton.

This is an exposed stitch, so be careful to carry your thread in the back *only* under the canvas mesh, following the numbering in the diagram very carefully.

Alicia Lace is stitched horizontally across the row from right to left over 1 horizontal and 1 vertical canvas thread.

Again, remember to follow the numbering on the diagram *exactly*.

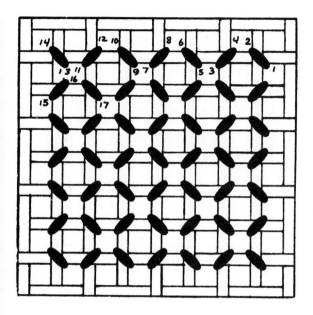

ARROWHEAD

The sample is worked on #14 Zweigart® Mono canvas with DMC® Floralia® (3-ply Persian yarn).

The Arrowhead is a combination of Milanese (page 100) and tent stitches worked in horizontal rows (**1-2, 3-4, 5-6, 7-8, 9-10, 11-12,** etc.).

The tent stitches are made after the arrowheads are completed.

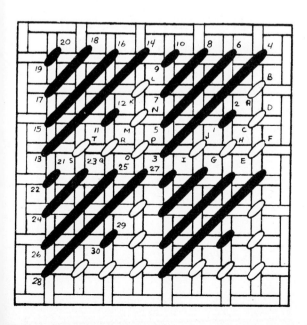

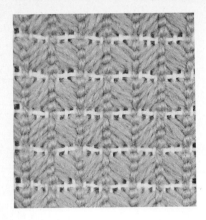

ARROWHEAD FLY

The sample is worked on #12 Zweigart® Mono canvas with DMC® Floralia® (3-ply Persian yarn).

Work the same as for the Fly stitch (page 69), in vertical rows placing 1 small straight stitch between the arrowheads.

The return row is worked in the opposite direction.

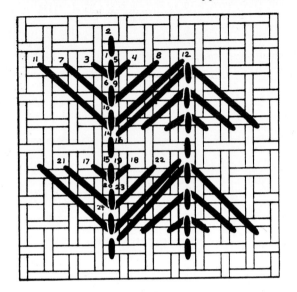

B

BACKSTITCH
(back)

The sample is worked on #12 Zweigart® Mono canvas with DMC® Floralia® (3-ply Persian yarn).

The Backstitch is usually used for outlining or to cover canvas threads that show between other stitches. It can also be worked in rows to cover a solid area.

This stitch is worked over 2 vertical canvas threads and back under 4 vertical canvas threads (2 of the last stitch and 2 empty or unworked threads). Turn the canvas for the next row.

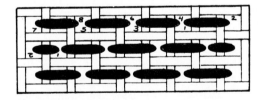

BARGELLO, SPLIT

The sample is worked on #10 Zweigart® Mono canvas with DMC® Floralia® (3-ply Persian yarn).

This stitch can be used with any bargello line pattern. Work the first row of the pattern over 2 horizontal canvas threads (**1-2, 3-4,** etc.). Then work the second row starting 1 horizontal canvas thread down, over 2 horizontal canvas threads, splitting the yarn of the previous row.

It is most often worked in 3 to 5 shades of the same color or overdyed variegated yarns.

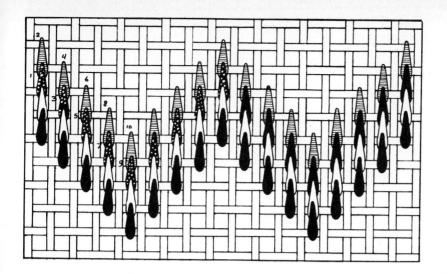

BARGELLO WAVE PATTERN

The sample is worked on Zweigart® Congress cloth with Anchor® floss.

This is an example of a 4-2 step pattern using the Gobelin stitches over 4 horizontal canvas threads. (See "Bargello," page 16).

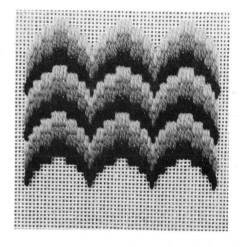

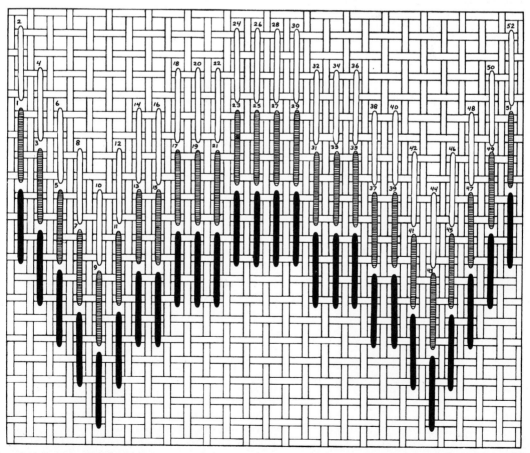

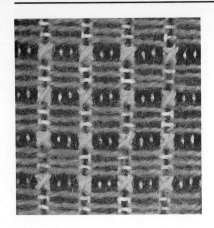

BARRED SQUARE
(broad cross)

The sample is worked on #10 Zweigart® Mono canvas with DMC® Floralia® (3-ply Persian yarn).

This is a combination of straight stitches worked vertically and horizontally over 4 canvas threads and a diagonal cross-stitch placed in the spaces between the squares.

First work a series of 3 vertical straight stitches over 4 horizontal canvas threads, leaving 2 vertical canvas threads between the groups of stitches (**1-2, 3-4, 5-6,** etc.).

Then lay a group of 3 horizontal straight stitches over these stitches covering 4 vertical canvas threads (**A-B, C-D, E-F,** etc.).

Finally, add the cross-stitch in the spaces between the squares over the 2 exposed horizontal and vertical canvas threads (**a-b, c-d, e-f,** etc.).

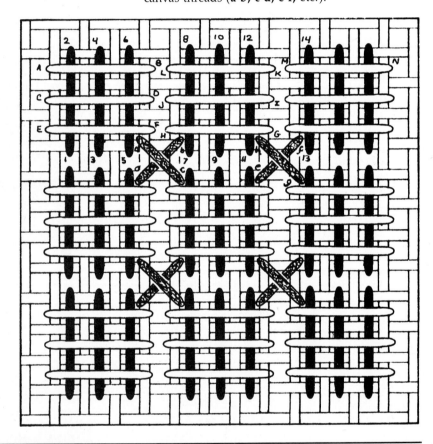

BASKET
(basket filling, wicker)

The sample is worked on #12 Zweigart® Mono canvas with Anchor® Tapisserie (tapestry yarn).

This stitch consists of alternating groups of vertical and horizontal straight stitches and looks like a woven basket. It covers large areas quickly. Be careful to use an even tension.

The first unit is composed of 3 upright stitches placed over 4 horizontal canvas threads. The second unit is composed of 3 horizontal stitches placed over 4 vertical canvas threads.

Work these two stitch units across the row. The return row is worked with vertical under horizontal and horizontal under vertical units (see diagram). The stitch count can vary—just remember the formula: 3 stitches over 4 canvas threads, 4 stitches over 5 canvas threads, 5 stitches over 6 canvas threads, etc.

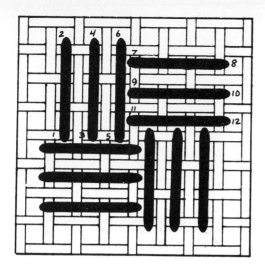

BAZAAR
(multicolor herringbone, six-color herringbone)

The sample is worked on #14 Zweigart® Mono canvas with DMC® Floralia® (3-ply Persian yarn).

This decorative woven stitch is worked *only* from left to right and is a very bulky stitch when worked with a normal weight yarn for the chosen canvas. I recommend using 1–2 strands of Persian-type yarn. It is also necessary to work with a loose tension to avoid buckling the canvas.

The stitch is worked over 4 horizontal and 4 vertical canvas threads. Follow the diagram exactly for the placement of the stitches.

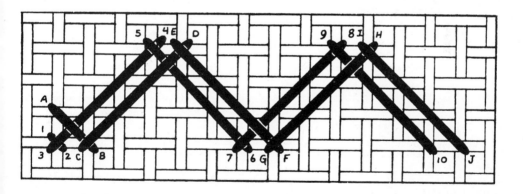

BEETLE

The sample is worked on #14 Zweigart® Mono canvas with DMC® Floralia® (3-ply Persian yarn).

The Beetle stitch is composed of 3 upright straight stitches with 8 varied-length horizontal straight stitches worked over them, producing an oval shape.

First, work the 3 upright straight stitches over 9 horizontal canvas threads (**1-2, 3-4, 5-6**). These stitches become a padding for the stitch. Next, work the 8 horizontal straight stitches: the first over 4 canvas threads (**7-8**); the second over 6 (**9-10**); the third, fourth, fifth, and sixth over 8 (**11-12, 13-14, 15-16, 17-18**); the seventh over 6 (**19-20**); and the last over 4 canvas threads (**21-22**).

I prefer to work this stitch on the diagonal, but it can be worked in horizontal rows.

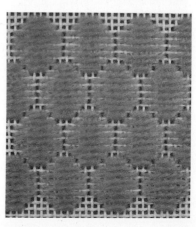

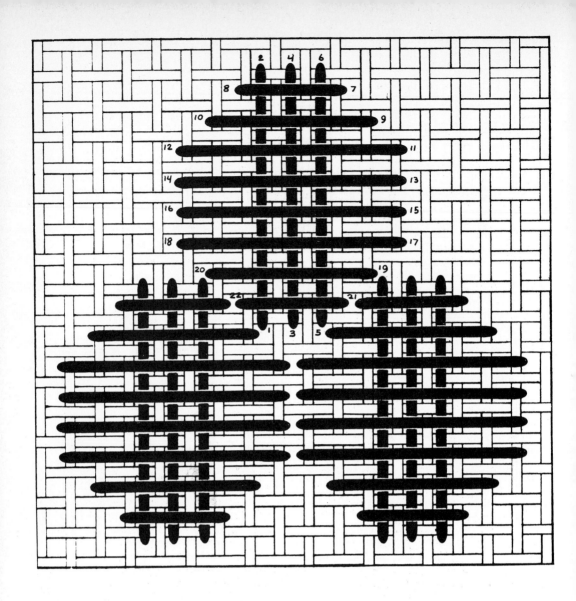

BEETLE, BARRED

The sample is stitched on #14 Zweigart® Mono canvas with DMC® Floralia® (3-ply Persian yarn).

This is a variation of the Beetle stitch. It consists of a group of 10 horizontal straight stitches with 3 vertical stitches worked over them.

Work the first stitch over 2 vertical canvas threads (**1-2**), the second over 4 vertical canvas threads (**3-4**), the third over 6 (**5-6**), the fourth to seventh over 8 vertical canvas threads, the eighth over 6, the ninth over 4, and finally the tenth stitch over 2 vertical canvas threads.

The 3 vertical stitches are worked over these 10 stitches, starting at the base, 1 horizontal canvas thread below the last stitch, and over 11 horizontal canvas threads and into the center hole at the top of the Beetle stitch (**A-B**).

Start the second stitch in the same hole as the first stitch (**A**) and return 1 horizontal and 1 vertical canvas thread to the left, over 10 stitches (**A-C**). The third stitch is worked in the same way, but 1 vertical and 1 horizontal stitch to the right (**A-D**).

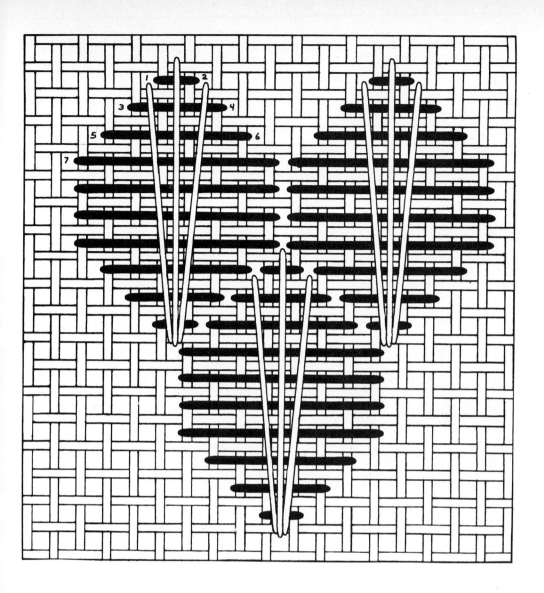

BOKHARA COUCHING, RANDOM
(bamboo)

The sample is worked on #12 Zweigart® Mono canvas with Anchor® Tapisserie (tapestry yarn).

To work this stitch, a long length of yarn is laid from left to right over any number of vertical canvas threads (**1-2**). It is then couched or tied on the return trip over the yarn and 1 horizontal canvas thread spaced in a random manner (**3-4, 5-6,** etc.). *No pattern is created or repeated.*

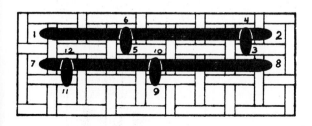

BOKHARA COUCHING, STRIPE PATTERN
(bamboo pattern)

The sample is worked on #12 Zweigart® Mono canvas with Anchor® Tapisserie (tapestry yarn).

This stitch is worked exactly like the Random Bokhara Couching stitch, until the tie-down stitches are worked on the return trip. These stitches are placed in a repeat pattern of your choice.

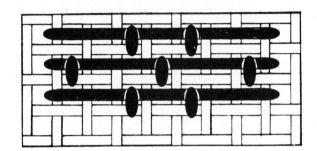

BOKHARA COUCHING, TIED

The sample is worked on #12 Zweigart® Mono canvas with DMC® Floralia® (3-ply Persian yarn).

The Bokhara Couching stitch can be worked in a number of ways. In this method, a long length of yarn is laid across any number of vertical canvas threads (**1-2**). On the return trip, a small tent stitch is worked across the yarn and the *intersection* of 1 vertical and 1 horizontal canvas thread (**3-4, 5-6**). These tent stitches can be worked in any pattern of your choice; however, it is advisable to leave no more than 4 vertical canvas threads between tent stitches.

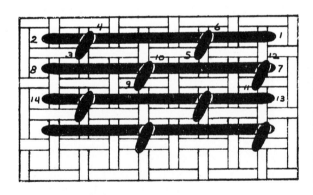

BOWTIE
(bow, lone tied star)

The sample is worked on #18 Zweigart® Mono canvas with DMC® Floralia® (3-ply Persian yarn).

This is a combination of the Bowtie on a background of tent or cross-stitches.

Start by making a diagonal stitch over 3 horizontal and 3 vertical canvas threads (**1-2**). Cross this with a diagonal stitch over 1 horizontal and 3 vertical canvas threads (**3-4**). Next, cross both stitches with a stitch over 3 horizontal and 1 vertical canvas threads (**5-6**). Finally, tie all 3 stitches with a tiny tie stitch (**7-8**). Fill in the background with tent or cross-stitches.

Since this stitch stands alone, it can be worked as a surface motif any place desired. It is not necessary to follow the diagram for Bowtie placement.

BRICK

The sample is worked on #10 Zweigart® Mono canvas with Anchor® Tapisserie (tapestry yarn).

This is an easy vertical straight stitch pattern worked over 2 horizontal canvas threads stepped 1 thread up and 1 thread down across the row (**1-2, 3-4, 5-6, 7-8,** etc.).

The Brick pattern can be worked in 1 or 2 colors.

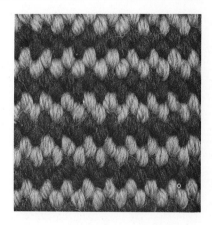

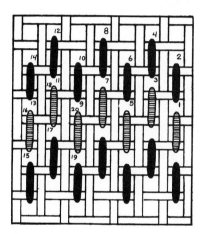

BRICK, DOUBLE

The sample is worked on #14 Zweigart® Mono canvas with Anchor® Tapisserie (tapestry yarn).

This is a variation of the Giant Brick pattern, worked double over 4 canvas threads (**1-2, 3-4**), stepped 2 canvas threads up and down (**5-6, 7-8**). Work this pattern in 2 colors.

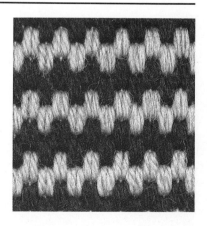

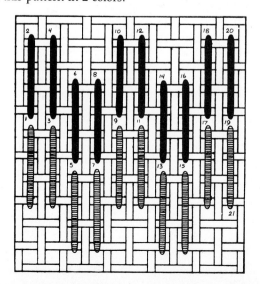

BRICK, FILLING

The sample is worked on #10 Zweigart® Mono canvas with Anchor® Tapisserie (tapestry yarn).

This stitch forms an allover pattern that resembles a brick wall.

The bricks are made of 2 long horizontal stitches worked over 4 vertical canvas threads (**1-2, 3-4**). The mortar is represented by a vertical backstitch worked between the bricks over 2 horizontal canvas threads (**A-B, C-D,** etc.).

The stitch can be worked in horizontal rows or on the diagonal as shown in the diagram. First, work the long horizontal stitches. Next, add the backstitches in a different color or texture thread.

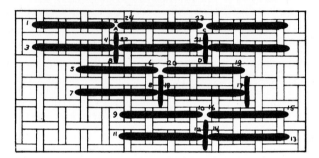

BRICK, GIANT

The sample is worked on #10 Zweigart® Mono canvas with Anchor® Tapisserie (tapestry yarn).

This is a variation of the Brick pattern, worked over 4 horizontal canvas threads stepped 2 canvas threads up and down.

Work 2 rows in each color.

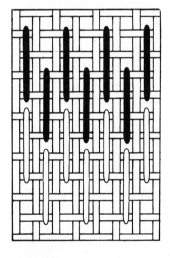

BRICKING

The sample is worked on #10 Zweigart® Mono canvas with Anchor® Tapisserie (tapestry yarn).

This is a variation of the Brick stitch. It is made of blocks of 3 horizontal stitches worked over 3 vertical canvas threads in the first row (**1-2, 3-4, 5-6, 7-8,** etc.). The second row alternates blocks of 2 vertical stitches worked over 3 horizontal canvas threads (**19-20, 21-22,** etc.).

Repeat these 2 rows for the pattern.

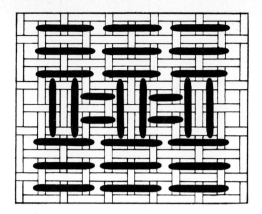

BULLION KNOT
(caterpillar, coil, worm, porto rico rose, grub knot)

The sample is worked on #18 Zweigart® Mono canvas with #5 DMC® perle cotton.

The Bullion Knot is used as an accent stitch or worked closely together to create a dense textured filling.

The weight of the thread or yarn will determine the size of the finished Bullion Knot. *Using a thick needle with a small eye will make it easier to work this stitch.*

Method 1
Bring the thread or yarn to the front at **1** and insert the needle into the canvas a few canvas threads away, at **2**, with the tip of the needle returning to the front at the beginning point **1**. The space (number of vertical canvas threads) between the point where the needle is inserted into the canvas and the point where the tip of the needle returns to the front will determine the length of the Bullion Knot.

Next, wrap the thread or yarn around the tip of the needle 5–8 times. Pull the needle gently through the wrapped thread, holding it firmly with the thumb and forefinger as you pull.

Finally, pull the yarn in the opposite direction to tighten the bullion and insert the needle back into the canvas at the start of the stitch at **2**. The stitch should lie in a straight line on the surface of the canvas.

To create a wormy or bumpy Bullion Knot, wrap the yarn around the needle many more times than the length of the bullion. (See Diagram A.)

A

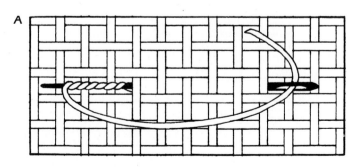

B

C

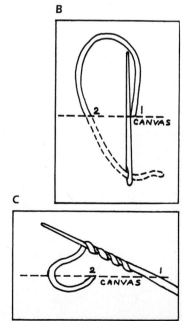

Method 2
This method is easier when using a frame.

1. Bring the needle up at **1** and down at **2** at the point where the bullion ends, leaving a loop of yarn on the top side of the canvas.
2. Bring the needle up again at **1** (Diagram B).
3. Take the loop of yarn as it comes from point **1** and wind it around the needle enough times to cover the distance from **1** to **2** (Diagram C).

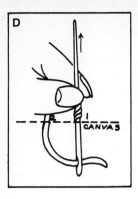 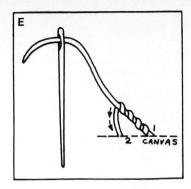 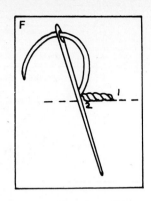

4. Hold the coil of yarn between the thumb and fore-finger (Diagram D) and pull the needle and yarn through the coil (Diagram E), pushing the coil back toward point **1** until the bullion is smooth.
5. Insert the needle back into the canvas at point **2** (Diagram F).

BUTTONHOLE

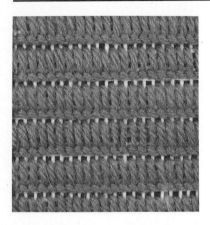

The sample is worked on #12 Zweigart® Mono canvas with Anchor® Tapisserie (tapestry yarn).

This is the simplest form of the Buttonhole stitch. There are many variations but this is the most often used.

Working from left to right across the canvas, place a vertical straight stitch over 3 or more horizontal canvas threads. (The diagram is worked over 4 horizontal canvas threads.)

The first stitch is made by bringing the yarn from the back to the front at the lower left-hand corner. Then insert the needle 4 horizontal canvas threads above this starting point and come back out at the starting point over the loop of yarn formed. Pull on the yarn firmly to complete the stitch. Work across the row following the diagram.

Row 2 starts 3 horizontal canvas threads above the first, overlapping the top of the stitches of the first row.

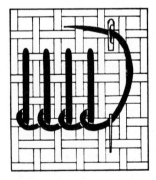

BYZANTINE

The sample is worked on #12 Zweigart® Mono canvas using DMC® Floralia® (3-ply Persian yarn).

The Byzantine stitch is worked diagonally over 2–4 horizontal and vertical canvas threads in a stepped pattern traditionally consisting of 5 stitches.

This stitch count can vary if you desire. The Byzantine stitch can be worked in 1 color as a background pattern or 2 or more colors as a border or frame.

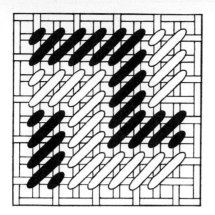

BYZANTINE, GRADUATED
(irregular Byzantine)

The sample is worked on #12 Zweigart® Mono canvas with DMC® Floralia® (3-ply Persian yarn).

The Byzantine is a large stepped diagonal stitch that is used to fill large areas. The Graduated Byzantine variation is worked over 1, 2, 3, and then 4 canvas threads in graduating colors or shades of the same color.

Start by working a row of tent stitches over 1 horizontal and 1 vertical canvas threads in steps of 6 stitches (**1-2, 3-4, 5-6**, etc.), using the lightest color.

Next, work a row of diagonal stitches over 2 horizontal and 2 vertical canvas threads directly beneath

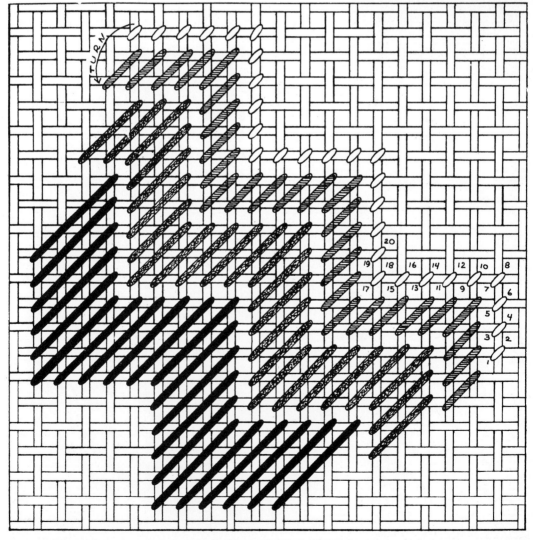

the first row (**A-B, C-D, E-F,** etc.), using the medium-light color.

Row 3 is worked over 3 horizontal and 3 vertical canvas threads using the medium color, and Row 4 is worked over 4 horizontal and 4 vertical canvas threads in the dark tone.

Repeat these 4 rows for the pattern.

BYZANTINE SCOTCH

The sample is worked on #14 Zweigart® Mono canvas with DMC® Floralia® (3-ply Persian yarn).

This stitch is a combination of the Byzantine steps worked over 3 horizontal and 3 vertical canvas threads (**1-2, 3-4, 5-6,** etc.) and a Scotch stitch (page 130) filling in between the steps in the same or a contrasting color (**A-B, C-D, E-F, G-H, I-J,** etc.).

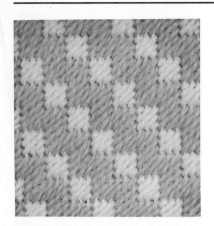

C

CASHMERE

The sample is worked on #10 Zweigart® Mono canvas with DMC® Floralia® (3-ply Persian yarn).

The Cashmere stitch is an extended Mosaic stitch (page 104) that is usually used to cover large background areas. Each unit is made of 4 diagonal stitches. This stitch may be worked in horizontal, vertical, or diagonal rows.

To work the Cashmere stitch in horizontal rows, begin at the base of the unit; to work vertical rows, begin at the top of the unit. Start the first stitch of the vertical row at the arrow marked **B**; the first stitch of an ascending diagonal row at the arrow marked **C**; the first stitch of a descending diagonal row at the arrow marked **D**; and the first stitch of a horizontal row at the arrow marked **A**.

This stitch will distort the canvas and should be worked on a frame.

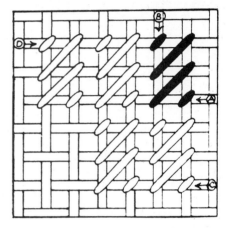

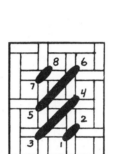

CASHMERE, CHECKER

The sample is worked on #12 Zweigart® Mono canvas with Anchor® Tapisserie (tapestry yarn).

This stitch alternates the Cashmere stitch with the tent stitch. It can be worked horizontally, vertically, or diagonally.

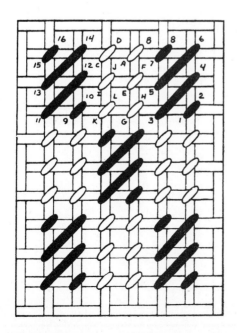

CASHMERE, DIAGONAL
(continuous cashmere)

The sample is worked on #12 Zweigart® Mono canvas with DMC® Floralia® (3-ply Persian yarn).

The Cashmere stitch is a wonderful background or filling stitch. Worked diagonally, it creates a pattern by itself that is particularly suited to depict water or rolling hills.

Each Diagonal Cashmere stitch unit consists of 3, not 4, diagonal stitches as for the regular Cashmere stitch.

Most stitches worked on the diagonal tend to distort the canvas and require extensive blocking; therefore, it is advisable to use a frame and the stab method of stitching when working large areas.

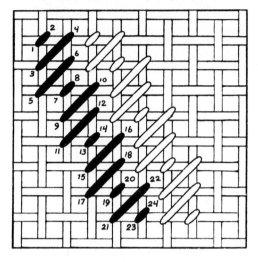

CASHMERE, ELONGATED

The sample is worked on #12 Zweigart® Mono canvas with Anchor® Tapisserie (tapestry yarn).

This is a variation of the Cashmere stitch with any number of long stitches (over 2 horizontal and 2 vertical canvas threads) inserted in the middle of the stitch.

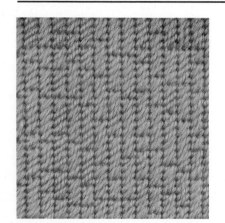

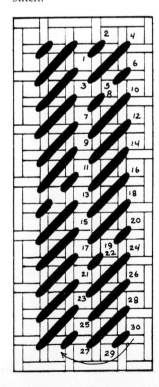

Begin with 1 tent stitch over an intersection of 1 vertical and 1 horizontal canvas thread (**1-2**). Next work any number of center stitches over 2 horizontal and 2 vertical canvas threads (**3-4, 5-6, 7-8,** etc.). End with a tent stitch.

Continue to work vertically to finish the row.

CASHMERE, FRAMED

The sample is worked on #10 Zweigart® Mono canvas with Anchor® Tapisserie (tapestry yarn).

Work blocks of the Cashmere stitch (**1-2, 3-4, 5-6, 7-8**) across the row, leaving 1 canvas thread between the blocks. Leave 1 horizontal canvas thread between the rows.

Fill in these blank rows with Continental Tent (page 144) stitches in the same or a contrasting color.

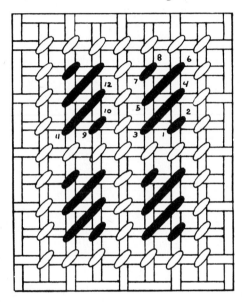

CASHMERE, TIED

The sample is worked on #12 Zweigart® Mono canvas with Anchor® Tapisserie (tapestry yarn) and Anchor® 6-strand floss.

This is a variation of the Cashmere stitch with a tied stitch added in a second color bringing the 2 longer stitches together.

Start by working a series of Cashmere stitches across the area to be covered. The diagram is worked on the diagonal (**1-2, 3-4, 5-6, 7-8**).

When the Cashmere stitches are completed, work a tied stitch over the 2 longer stitches (**3-4, 5-6,** etc.). It may be necessary to move the stitches aside to find the holes to place the tied stitches (white stitches on the diagram).

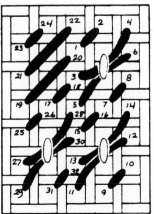

CHAIN

The sample is worked on #12 Zweigart® Mono canvas with DMC® Floralia® (3-ply Persian yarn).

The Chain stitch can be worked in a vertical row, as a solid area filling, on a curve, and with a tent stitch between the rows to form a ridged variation.

Start with a vertical row with the yarn and needle coming to the front at **1** (see Diagram A). Make a loop and insert the needle back into **1** and under 2 horizontal canvas threads, coming out at **2**. Holding the loop with the left thumb, pull the yarn gently to the front. The first loop is now complete. Repeat these steps to work a vertical row.

A 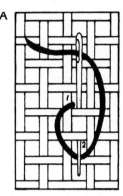 **B**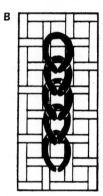

CHAIN, DETACHED

The sample is worked on #12 Zweigart® Mono canvas with DMC® Floralia® (3-ply Persian yarn).

The Detached Chain is simply a single Chain stitch that can be worked in any direction on the surface of the canvas. Always work a small stitch at the base of the loop to anchor the stitch down to the canvas. (See diagram.)

CHECKER, LARGE
(checkerboard, chequer)

The sample is worked on #12 Zweigart® Mono canvas with Anchor® Tapisserie (tapestry yarn) and Anchor® floss.

The Large Checker stitch is a combination of the Scotch stitch (page 130) and the tent stitch worked in alternating squares. The Scotch stitch is worked diagonally, leaving the correct number of canvas threads between the rows to be worked later with the tent stitches.

This stitch can be worked in 1 color to create a surface texture or in 2 colors for an allover pattern.

As with most slanting stitches, a frame should be used to work this stitch.

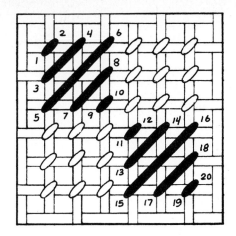

CHECKER, SMALL

The sample is worked on #12 Zweigart® Mono canvas with DMC® Floralia® (3-ply Persian yarn).

The Small Checker stitch is a combination of the Diagonal Mosaic stitch (page 105) and the tent stitch worked in alternating squares. Follow the same working order as in the Large Checker stitch.

This stitch can be worked in 1 color as a surface texture or in 2 colors to create an allover pattern.

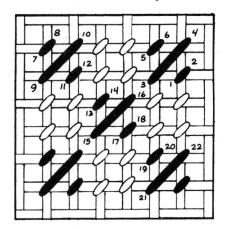

CHINESE
(Pekinese)

The sample is worked on #14 Zweigart® Mono canvas with Anchor® Tapisserie (tapestry yarn).

The Chinese stitch can be used for a single line or for an allover pattern.

First, work a row of backstitches over 3–5 vertical canvas threads. Then, using a yarn of the same or a contrasting color, weave over and under the backstitches, following the direction of the arrows in the diagram. Use a moderate tension to weave over the backstitches.

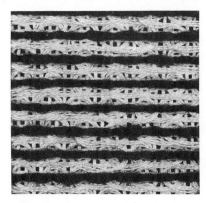

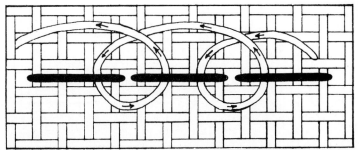

CHINESE KNOT
(Pekin knot, blind knot)

The sample is worked on #18 Zweigart® Mono canvas with DMC® Floralia® (3-ply Persian yarn).

The Chinese Knot resembles the French Knot (page 72) but is flatter in appearance. It is usually worked as a single decorative surface stitch, but can be stitched as a solid textured area.

The weight of the thread or yarn will determine the size of the finished knot.

To work, bring the yarn to the front of the canvas at **A**. Make a loop of yarn around the needle and insert it 1 horizontal canvas thread above, at **B**. The tip of the needle should return to the front at the place where the next stitch is to be worked.

Hold the loop with the thumb and pull the needle through to the front to tighten the knot.

Work the rows right to left only. Fit the second row between the stitches of the row above.

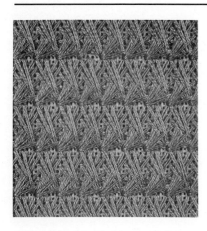

CRISSCROSS

The sample is worked on Zweigart® Congress cloth with Anchor® 6-strand floss.

This complicated stitch produces a lacy texture. It is a large stitch that covers 10 horizontal and 12 vertical canvas threads.

Always work this stitch from left to right, following the numbering on the diagram *exactly*.

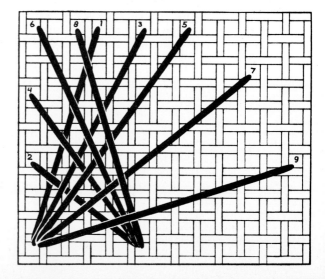

CROSS

The sample is worked on #14 Zweigart® Mono canvas with Anchor® Tapisserie (tapestry yarn).

This is the most popular and well-known stitch used on fabric and canvas.

Diagram A shows the single complete stitch or unit worked over 2 horizontal and 2 vertical canvas threads.

For a row or large area, it is preferable to work a row of half-cross stitches and then return, crossing the half-crosses in the opposite direction. Always make sure the top stitch of each cross points in the same direction.

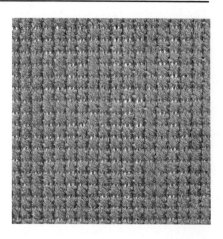

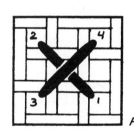

A

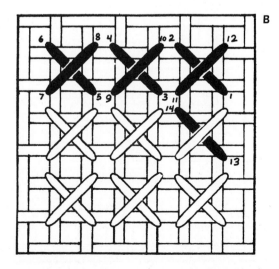

B

CROSS, BRAIDED

The sample is worked on #14 Zweigart® Mono canvas and DMC® Floralia® (3-ply Persian yarn).

The Braided Cross-Stitch combines the Cross-Stitch, the Diagonal stitch (page 77), and the French Knot (page 72).

First, work the diagonal stitches over 2 horizontal and 2 vertical canvas threads following the numbering on the diagram (**1-2, 3-4, 5-6, 7-8**). Note that in working **7-8** you must slip the needle *under* stitch **1-2**.

Next, work the cross-stitches over the intersections of 1 horizontal and 1 vertical canvas thread.

Finally, work the French knots in the center of the braided stitches.

CROSS, DIAGONAL UPRIGHT

The sample is worked on #12 Zweigart® Mono canvas with Anchor® Tapisserie (tapestry yarn).

The Diagonal Upright Cross-Stitch is a woven upright offset cross worked on the diagonal.

Begin by working a vertical stitch over 3 horizontal canvas threads (**1-2**). Cross this stitch with a horizontal stitch over 3 vertical canvas threads (**3-4**).

Repeat these 2 stitches, working diagonally across the area to be stitched, (**5-6, 7-8, 9-10, 11-12,** etc.).

Repeat each row in a different color, forming diagonal stripes (**A-B, C-D,** etc.; **a-b, c-d,** etc.).

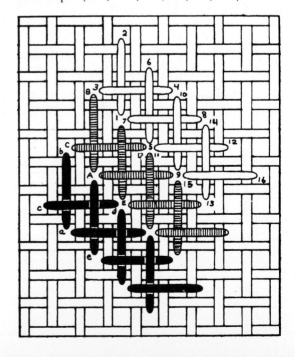

CROSS, DOUBLE PLAITED

The sample is worked on #12 Zweigart® Mono canvas with Anchor® Tapisserie (tapestry yarn).

This is a variation on the Cross-Stitch. Follow the numbers on the diagram exactly.

First, work a long vertical straight stitch over 7 horizontal canvas threads (**1-2**). Add a horizontal straight stitch over 7 vertical canvas threads (**3-4**).

Next, place another vertical straight stitch next to the first stitch (**5-6**) and another horizontal straight stitch next to the second stitch (**7-8**). (See Diagram A.)

Finally, work the diagonal stitches. Start 2 vertical canvas threads to the left of the first stitch to work the first diagonal stitch (**9-10**). Repeat, starting 2 vertical canvas threads to the right of the third stitch (**11-12**). (See Diagram B.)

Diagram C shows the placement of the final 2 diagonal stitches (**13-14** and **15-16**). Notice that the last stitch (**15-16**) is slipped *under* rather than over stitch **9-10**.

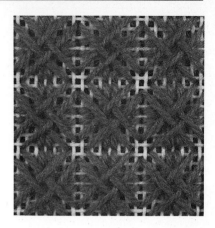

A

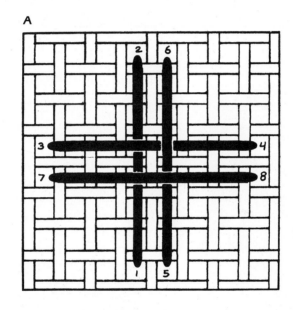

B   **C**

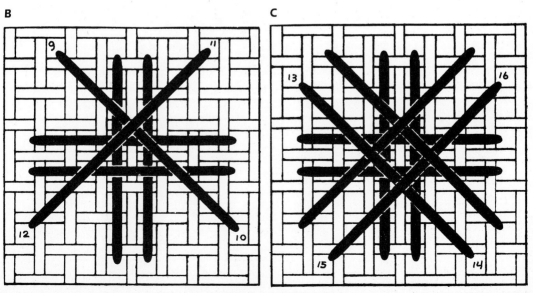

CROSS, HITCHED

The sample is worked on #10 Zweigart® Mono canvas with DMC® Floralia® (3-ply Persian yarn) and Anchor® floss.

This stitch is a combination of cross-stitches worked over 3 horizontal and 2 vertical canvas threads (**1-2, 3-4, 5-6, 7-8**, etc.) and crossed with a diagonal stitch in a second color (**A-B, C-D**, etc.).

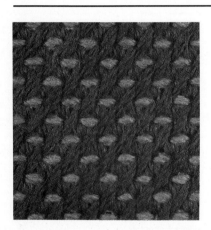

CROSS, HOURGLASS

The sample is worked on #12 Zweigart® Mono canvas with DMC® Floralia® (3-ply Persian yarn).

The Hourglass Cross-Stitch is worked on the diagonal in a stepped pattern.

Start by placing a diagonal stitch over 2 vertical and 4 horizontal canvas threads (**1-2**). Then, step down 6 horizontal canvas threads to start the second stitch (**3-4**). Continue to the end of the area to be covered. The return trip completes each cross (**7-8, 9-10**, etc.).

The top and bottom of the hourglass are stitched in a different or lighter shade of the same color over 2 vertical canvas threads.

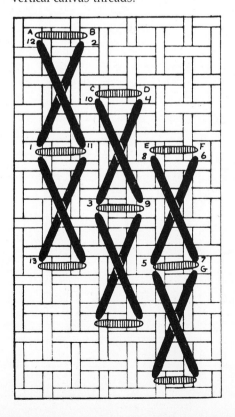

CROSS, OVERLAPPED OBLONG
(encroaching oblong cross, overlapping oblong cross)

The sample is worked on #12 Zweigart® Mono canvas with Anchor® Tapisserie (tapestry yarn).

The Overlapped Oblong Cross resembles a plaited stitch. Each row of crosses is worked half the length of the cross over the cross of the previous row. These rows are worked horizontally.

This stitch can be worked in a single color or graduated shades of 1 color.

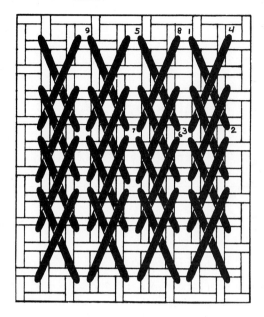

CROSS, PLAITED
(interlaced cross)

The sample is worked on #14 Zweigart® Mono canvas with Anchor® Tapisserie (tapestry yarn) and #5 DMC perle cotton.

This stitch consists of a Cross-Stitch interlaced with yarn of the same or a different color.

First, work the cross-stitches over 4 horizontal and 4 vertical canvas threads (**1-2, 3-4, 5-6, 7-8,** etc.). Then come up from the back at **A** and weave over each leg of the cross, slipping the yarn *under* each leg at the corners, except for the last leg. Continue around, returning to the back at **B**.

Repeat for each cross.

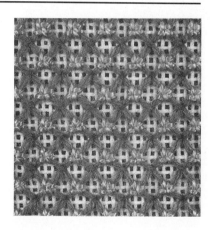

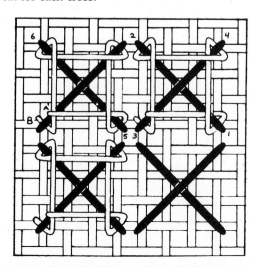

CROSS, ROMAN
(twelve)

The sample is worked on #10 Zweigart® Mono canvas with DMC® Floralia® (3-ply Persian yarn).

This stitch is a combination of a Cross-Stitch and 2 vertical straight stitches, giving the appearance of the Roman numeral twelve.

Work the cross horizontally across the row (**1-2, 3-4,** etc.), returning to complete the cross (**5-6, 7-8,** etc.).

Next, fill in the spaces with groups of 2 vertical straight stitches (**A-B, C-D, E-F,** etc.).

Work this stitch in 1 color.

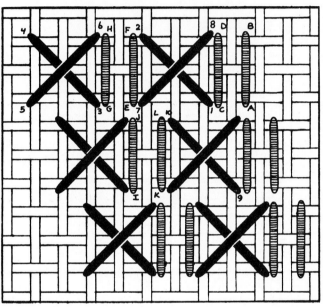

CROSS, UPRIGHT
(straight cross)

The sample is worked on #10 Zweigart® Mono canvas with Anchor® Tapisserie (tapestry yarn).

The Upright Cross-Stitch is traditionally worked as a single unit crossing over 2 horizontal and then 2 vertical canvas threads.

The second row is staggered between the stitches of the first row, interlocking the rows as you work.

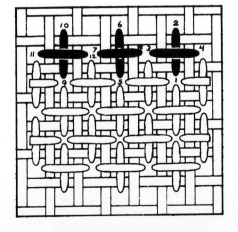

CROSS, WOVEN

The sample is worked on #14 Zweigart® Mono canvas with DMC® Floralia® (3-ply Persian yarn)

The Woven Cross-Stitch can be worked over 3 or 4 horizontal and vertical canvas threads.

First, work 3 identical legs of the cross *over* one another as shown in the diagram. The last leg is woven *under* the first leg of the first cross.

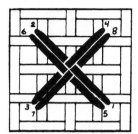

CROSS AND HALF-CROSS VARIATION #1

The sample is worked on #10 Zweigart® Mono canvas with Anchor® Tapisserie (tapestry yarn).

This is a pattern of small cross-stitches alternating with tent stitches separated by a row of tent stitches.

First work a row of tent stitches (**1-2, 3-4, 5-6,** etc.). Make the return trip crossing *every other* stitch (**17-18, 19-20,** etc.).

Next make a row of tent stitches. Repeat these 2 rows for the pattern.

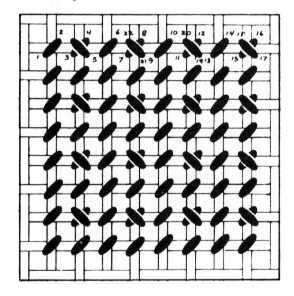

CROSS AND HALF-CROSS VARIATION #2

The sample is worked on #10 Zweigart® Mono canvas with DMC® Floralia® (3-ply Persian yarn).

This combination of small cross-stitches and tent stitches is worked in horizontal rows.

Start by working the tent stitches (**1-2, 3-4, 5-6,** etc.) across the row. Make the return trip crossing *every other* stitch (**15-16, 17-18,** etc.).

Repeat for each row.

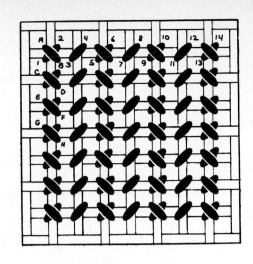

CROSS AND HALF-CROSS VARIATION #3

The sample is worked on #10 Zweigart® Mono canvas with DMC® Floralia® (3-ply Persian yarn).

This variation of the Cross and Half-Cross 1 is worked in alternating horizontal rows of cross-stitches (**1-2, 3-4,** etc.) and tent stitches.

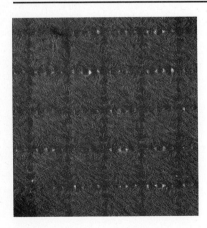

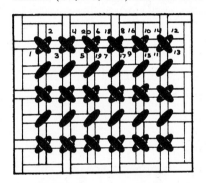

CROSS I, BOUND

The sample is worked on #10 Zweigart® Mono canvas with DMC® Floralia® (3-ply Persian yarn).

The Bound Cross I is worked horizontally across the row.

Start with a diagonal stitch over 3 horizontal and 3 vertical canvas threads (**1-2**). Next, make a diagonal stitch starting 1 horizontal canvas thread down over 4 horizontal and 4 vertical canvas threads (**3-4**). Then work another diagonal stitch starting 1 vertical canvas thread to the right over 3 horizontal and 3 vertical canvas threads (**5-6**).

The top layer is worked *over* the first group of 3 stitches in the opposite direction (**7-8, 9-10, 11-12**).

Work across the row, completing each block before starting the next.

CROSS II, BOUND

The sample is worked on #12 Zweigart® Mono canvas with Anchor® Tapisserie (tapestry yarn).

The Bound Cross II is worked by layers across the row.

Start with a diagonal stitch over 3 horizontal and 3 vertical canvas threads (**1-2**). Finish the bottom layer of stitches (**3-4, 5-6**).

Work this group of 3 stitches across the row (**7-8, 9-10, 11-12,** etc.). Complete all base layer stitches in the darker color.

The return trip is worked vertically or horizontally in a lighter color (**A-B, C-D, E-F,** etc.).

CROSSED CROSSES
(fancy cross)

The sample is worked on #14 Zweigart® Mono canvas with DMC® Floralia® (3-ply Persian yarn).

This stitch is a combination of large Smyrna crosses (page 137) and smaller cross-stitches worked in 2 colors, forming an interesting texture pattern.

Start by working a horizontal row of large Smyrna crosses over 4 horizontal and 4 vertical canvas threads (**1-2, 3-4, 5-6, 7-8**).

Then, using the second color, work the small crosses over 2 horizontal and 2 vertical canvas threads (**A-B, C-D, E-F,** etc.).

CROSSED DIAMOND

The sample is worked on #10 Zweigart® Mono canvas with DMC® Floralia® (3-ply Persian yarn) and Anchor® floss.

The Crossed Diamond stitch is worked in 2 or 3 colors or 2 different threads (yarn or floss, etc.).

Start with the darker color and work 4 straight stitches over 3 canvas threads (**1-2, 3-4, 5-6, 7-8**).

Next, work the 2 diagonal stitches on each side of these 4 straight stitches (**9-10, 11-12**), (**13-14, 15-16**), (**17-18, 19-20**), (**21-22, 23-24**).

Continue by working the 4 alternating tent stitches in the same color yarn (**25-26, 27-28, 29-30, 31-32**).

Repeat for each square of the diamond.

Finally, using a different color or thread, work the backstitches (**a-b, c-d**, etc.).

CROSSES, STAGGERED

The sample is worked on #12 Zweigart® Mono canvas with DMC® Floralia® (3-ply Persian yarn).

The Staggered Crosses are worked diagonally in 1 or 2 colors.

Start by working across 2 horizontal and 2 vertical canvas threads, stepping 1 canvas thread down and 1 canvas thread to the right (**1-2, 3-4, 5-6**, etc.). Return, completing each cross working uphill.

Following the diagram, work the smaller crosses across the intersections of 1 vertical and 1 horizontal canvas thread (**A-B, C-D**, etc.).

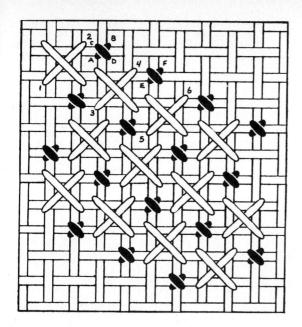

CROW'S FOOT

The sample is worked on #14 Zweigart® Mono canvas with Anchor® Tapisserie (tapestry yarn).

The Crow's Foot is worked over 3 horizontal and 4 vertical canvas threads.

Start by working 1 straight and 2 diagonal stitches radiating from 1 hole (**1, 2, 3**). Next, make a straight stitch over 3 horizontal canvas threads to separate the crow's foot stitches (**4-5**).

To separate the rows, work a Backstitch (page 26) over 4 vertical canvas threads (**A-B, C-D,** etc.).

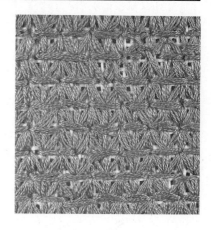

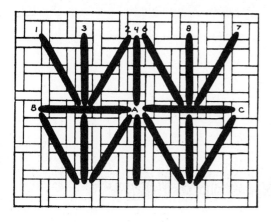

D

DAISIES, SQUARED
(eyelet, circular squared)

The sample is worked on #14 Zweigart® Mono canvas with Anchor® floss.

This is a variation of the Eye stitch (page 63). Large and small eyelets (daisies) are framed with backstitches.

One large and one small eyelet daisy are numbered in the diagram. Follow the numbering sequences carefully.

DAMASK

The sample is worked on #14 Zweigart® Mono canvas with Anchor® Tapisserie (tapestry yarn) and Anchor® floss.

This stitch can also be worked as a background stitch using 1 color and weight yarn for all the stitches, and would be worked on the diagonal. Both thin and thick stitches are stitched in the progression.

The Damask stitch is worked on the diagonal over 4 horizontal and 4 vertical canvas threads. This stitch leaves canvas exposed.

Count 8 horizontal canvas threads down and 4 vertical canvas threads to the right of the starting point. Make 1 diagonal stitch (**1-2**). Continue on the diagonal to the top right-hand corner.

The return journey is worked from upper right to lower left (**9-10, 11-12,** etc.).

After the pattern is completed (heavy stitches on diagram), work all the small stitches in a thinner, contrasting yarn over 2 horizontal canvas threads.

Compensating stitches have been diagramed.

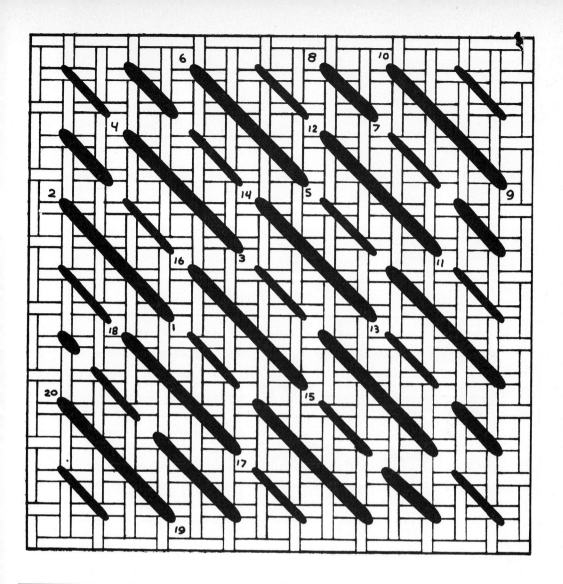

DAMASK DARNING

The sample is worked on #12 Zweigart® Mono canvas with Anchor® Tapisserie (tapestry yarn).

This stitch consists of 2 horizontal straight stitches worked over 4 vertical canvas threads (**1-2, 3-4,** etc.) across the row.

The second row is worked in a stepped manner, placing the 2 horizontal straight stitches 2 vertical canvas threads to the right of the beginning of the first row (**13-14, 15-16,** etc.).

Row 3 is placed directly under Row 1, forming a brick pattern.

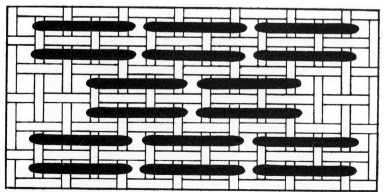

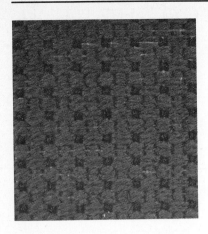

DAMASK DARNING WITH CROSS

The sample is worked on #14 Zweigart® Mono canvas with DMC® Floralia® (3-ply Persian yarn) and Anchor® floss.

This variation of the Damask Darning stitch alternates the block of 2 straight stitches with a small Cross-Stitch across the first row.

Work a row of 2 horizontal straight stitches (**1-2, 3-4**) over 4 vertical canvas threads, leaving 1 vertical canvas thread between the blocks of 2 stitches. This unworked thread will be covered later with a Cross-Stitch in another color.

For the second row, work 2 horizontal straight stitches over 2 vertical canvas threads (**9-10, 11-12**). Then work 2 horizontal straight stitches over 3 vertical canvas threads (**13-14, 15-16**). Repeat these 2 rows as shown in the diagram.

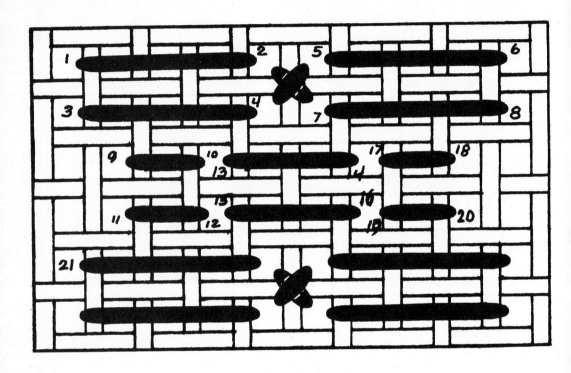

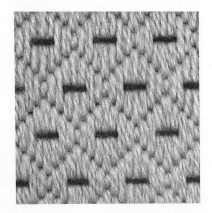

DARMSTADT PAVILION
(Darmstadt pattern)

The sample is worked on #14 Zweigart® Mono canvas with DMC® Floralia® (3-ply Persian yarn).

This stitch is worked in horizontal rows with ascending and descending vertical stitches forming a diamond pattern. The long horizontal stitch is placed in the center in a dark color after the diamonds are completed.

Start by working the upright stitches over 2, 4, and 6 horizontal canvas threads (**1-2, 3-4, 5-6**). Continue by working at the bottom of the diamond over 4, 5, and 4 horizontal canvas threads (**7-8, 9-10, 11-12**). Repeat these stitches at the top of the diamond (**13-14, 15-16, 17-18**). Complete the diamond by working the right side over 6, 4, and 2 horizontal canvas threads (**19-20, 21-22, 23-24**). Continue working the diamonds across the row.

When all the diamonds are finished, place the long horizontal stitch in the center of each diamond over 4 vertical canvas threads, using a dark color (**A-B, C-D,** etc.).

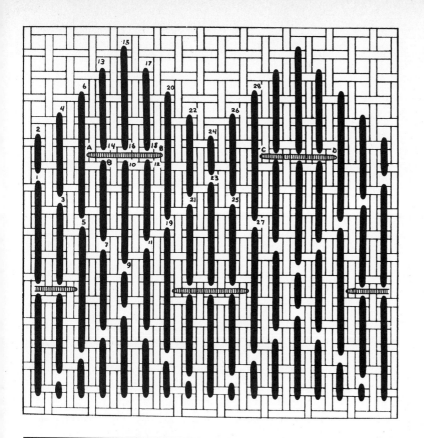

DIAMOND, STRAIGHT

The sample is worked on #14 Zweigart® Mono canvas with DMC® Floralia® (3-ply Persian yarn).

The Straight Diamond is a classic old stitch. It consists of the diamond shape made by working straight stitches over 1, 3, 5, 3, and 1 horizontal canvas threads (**1-2, 3-4, 5-6, 7-8,** etc.).

Next, work small vertical straight stitches over 1 horizontal canvas thread, outlining the diamonds and forming the pattern.

This stitch is worked in 1 color.

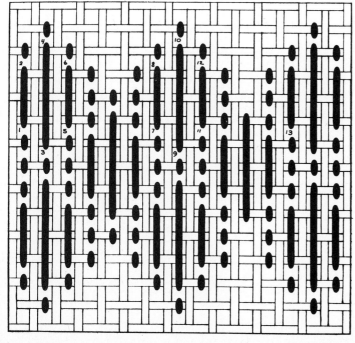

DIAMOND EYE
(diagonal star, diamond eyelet)

The sample is worked on #14 Zweigart® Mono canvas with DMC® Floralia® (3-ply Persian yarn).

The Diamond Eye is similar to the Eye stitch (page 63). Each leg of the diamond shape is worked from the outside *into* the center hole (**A** on the diagram). This stitch is worked in a counterclockwise direction. Every diamond unit begins at the side of the previous one.

DIAMOND RAY

The sample is worked on #14 Zweigart® Mono canvas with DMC® Floralia® (3-ply Persian yarn).

The Diamond Ray resembles a miniature leaf and can be used in that way as a decorative motif.

Work this stitch in horizontal rows across the area to be covered. Follow the numbering sequence on the diagram carefully.

DOUBLE

The sample is worked on #12 Zweigart® Mono canvas with DMC® Floralia® (3-ply Persian) and Anchor® Tapisserie (tapestry yarn).

This is a wonderful texture stitch worked in 2 different size crosses.

Start by working the larger crosses over 3 horizontal and 1 vertical canvas threads (**1-2, 3-4, 5-6,** etc.) across the row, skipping 1 vertical canvas thread between crosses.

The second row is worked *between* the crosses of the first row, starting over the bottom horizontal canvas thread of the first row (**17-18,** etc.).

Finally, in the same or a contrasting color, work the small crosses over the intersection of 1 horizontal and 1 vertical canvas thread between each large cross.

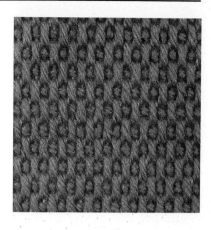

DOUBLE CROSS, TRAME

The sample is worked on #14 Zweigart® Mono canvas with Anchor® Tapisserie (tapestry yarn) and DMC® Floralia® (3-ply Persian yarn).

This stitch is worked in 2 colors, creating the illusion of a shadow behind the cross-stitches.

First work *all* the tramé stitches over the area to be covered (**A-B, C-D, E-F,** etc., and **a-b, c-d, e-f,** etc.).

To work the crosses across the intersections of the tramé stitches, stitch horizontally across the row with half-crosses (**1-2, 3-4, 5-6,** etc.).

Make the return trip completing each cross (**7-8, 9-10, 11-12,** etc.).

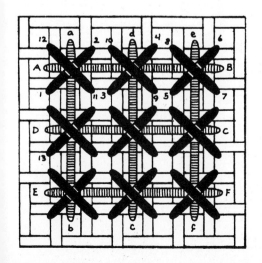

DOUBLE LEVIATHAN

The sample is worked on #12 Zweigart® Mono canvas with Anchor® Tapisserie (tapestry yarn).

The Double Leviathan stitch is used as a single decorative accent stitch or in rows to form a frame or background. Each stitch square creates a highly textured bump on the surface of the canvas.

The space allocated for this stitch *must* be divisible by 4, since this stitch cannot be halved or quartered as a compensation stitch.

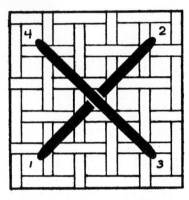 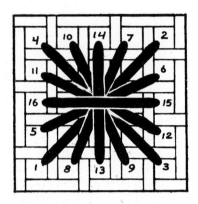

DUTCH

The sample is worked on #14 Zweigart® Mono canvas with DMC® Floralia® (3-ply Persian yarn).

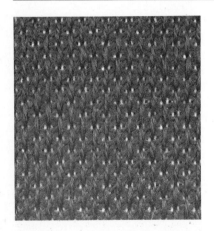

The Dutch stitch is a combination of the Oblong Cross-Stitch (page 49) worked horizontally over 2 horizontal and 4 vertical canvas threads (**1-2, 3-4**) and 1 upright straight stitch worked over the center of the cross over 4 horizontal canvas threads (**5-6**).

To cover a large area, first work the crosses in rows and then make the upright straight stitches on the return trip. The second and successive rows are fitted *between* the crosses of the row above, producing an allover interlocking pattern.

This pattern is particularly suitable to the use of two different textured threads: one for the cross and the other for the upright stitch.

E

ENGLISH

The sample is worked on #12 Zweigart® Mono canvas with DMC® Floralia® (3-ply Persian yarn).

The English stitch is worked over 4 horizontal and 6 vertical canvas threads.

First, work a unit of 5 upright straight stitches over 4 horizontal threads (**1-2, 3-4, 5-6, 7-8, 9-10**). Then, bring the needle up in the center hole on the bottom edge at **A** and down in the center hole on the right side at **B**.

Repeat on the left side, coming up at **C** and down at **D**. Now, put a diagonal stitch over each corner of the unit of upright straight stitches, working over 1 horizontal and 2 vertical canvas threads (see diagram).

This stitch is worked in horizontal rows.

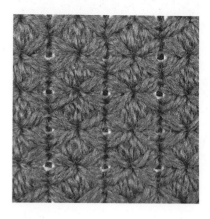

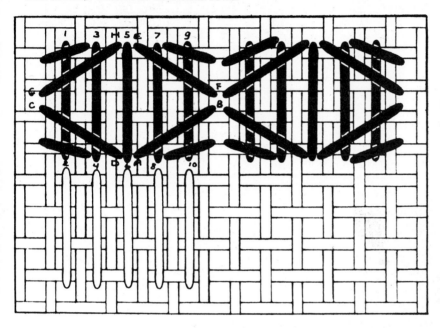

EYE
(eyelet)

The sample is worked on #14 Zweigart® Mono canvas with DMC® Floralia® (3-ply Persian yarn).

The eye stitch is usually worked over 4 horizontal and 4 vertical canvas threads but can be enlarged to 6 or 8 canvas threads.

A stitch is worked from each hole in a clockwise direction around the square *into* a center hole to form the eyelet.

This stitch can be used as a single decorative motif or worked in rows to form an allover pattern.

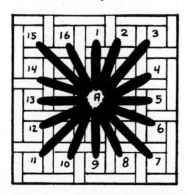

EYELET, REVERSED
(reversed eye)

The sample is worked on #14 Zweigart® Mono canvas with DMC® Floralia® (3-ply Persian yarn).

This stitch must be worked as an individual motif or in alternation with blocks of tent stitches. If this stitch is worked in a continuous row, the pattern will revert back to the normal eyelet stitch. It is worked over 6 horizontal and 6 vertical canvas threads.

Follow the diagram, completing each quarter of the stitch before going on to the next. Rotate the canvas one-quarter turn to the right and work the next quarter.

EYELET, SIX-SIDED
(six-sided eye)

The sample is worked on #14 Zweigart® Mono canvas with DMC® Floralia® (3-ply Persian yarn).

The Eyelet stitch can be worked in many different shapes, including the familiar square, rectangle, and circle. This unique variation forms a hexagonal shape. It is worked over 10 horizontal and 14 vertical canvas threads.

Begin by working 5 long straight stitches from the top edge, over 5 horizontal canvas threads into a center hole (**1-2-3-4-5**).

Then work 5 stitches down from the top edge to the left on a straight diagonal (**6-7-8-9-10**), each stitch ending in the center hole. Now repeat these 5 stitches

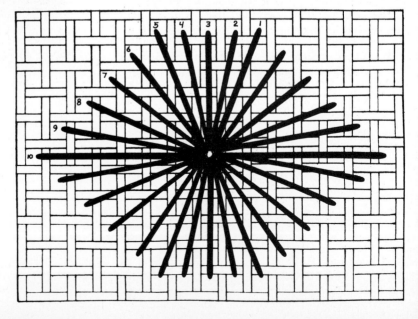

along the right side in a diagonal line as before (**11-12-13-14-15**).

The bottom half is worked as a reverse or mirror image of the top half.

This stitch can be used as an individual motif or as an allover pattern by working in vertical rows and fitting the second vertical row diagonal stitches into the diagonal stitches of the first row.

F

FAN
(ray)

The sample is worked on #10 Zweigart® Mono canvas with Anchor® Tapisserie (tapestry yarn).

The Fan stitch is one-quarter of the Eye stitch (page 63). It forms a square over 3, 4, or 5 canvas threads. You can vary this stitch by alternating the order of the stitches to **1-A, 7-A, 2-A, 6-A, 3-A, 5-A**, ending with **4-A**.

FERN

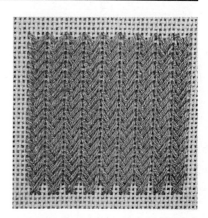

The sample is worked on Zweigart® Congress cloth with Anchor® floss.

The Fern stitch is a woven braid worked in vertical rows from top to bottom.

To work, come up from the back at **1** and down over 4 horizontal and 3 vertical canvas threads at **2**. Then, come up under 2 vertical canvas threads at **3** and down over 4 horizontal and 3 vertical canvas threads. Each subsequent unit is started 2 horizontal canvas threads below the first stitch of the last unit.

This stitch can be used to represent feathers or even foliage.

FISHBONE
(long and short oblique)

The sample is worked on #10 Zweigart® Mono canvas with Anchor® Tapisserie (tapestry yarn).

The Fishbone stitch is a tied diagonal stitch worked in vertical rows. The second vertical row of stitches slants in the opposite direction from the first row of stitches.

Start by working a long diagonal stitch over 4 horizontal and 4 vertical canvas threads (**1-2**). Next, tie the stitch with a tent stitch (**3-4**) as shown in the diagram.

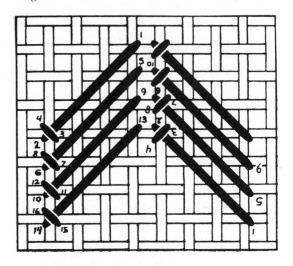

FISHBONE, HORIZONTAL

The sample is worked on #10 Zweigart® Mono canvas with Anchor® Tapisserie (tapestry yarn).

This version of the Fishbone stitch can be worked horizontally or vertically with the stitches forming vertical rows, or diagonally (see diagram) to form a diagonal stripe.

First, work a horizontal stitch over 4 vertical canvas threads (**1-2**). Then, make a small tie or tent stitch over the yarn and 1 horizontal and 1 vertical canvas thread (**3-4**).

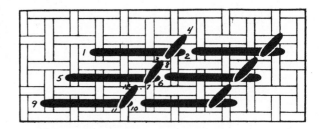

FLORAL

The sample is worked on #14 Zweigart® Mono canvas with DMC® Floralia® (3-ply Persian yarn).

This is a combination stitch worked in 2 horizontal rows to form the pattern.

The first row consists of 3 vertical Satin stitches (page 79) worked over 3 horizontal canvas threads (**1-2, 3-4, 5-6**) followed by a Cross-Stitch worked over 3 horizontal and 3 vertical canvas threads (**7-8, 9-10**).

The second row places 3 horizontal satin stitches worked over 3 vertical canvas threads alternating with a small cross-stitch worked over 2 horizontal and 2 vertical canvas threads.

Alternate the blocks of satin stitches and crosses.

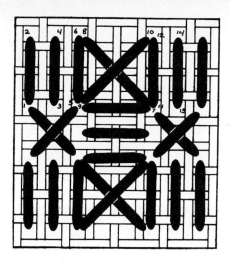

FLORENTINE FLAME
(bargello, flame)

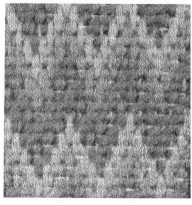

The sample is worked on #14 Zweigart® Mono canvas with Anchor® floss.

This pattern consists of a group of straight stitches worked over 4 horizontal canvas threads in ascending and then descending directions.

Each stitch is placed 2 canvas threads above or below the preceding stitch (**1-2, 3-4, 5-6,** etc.).

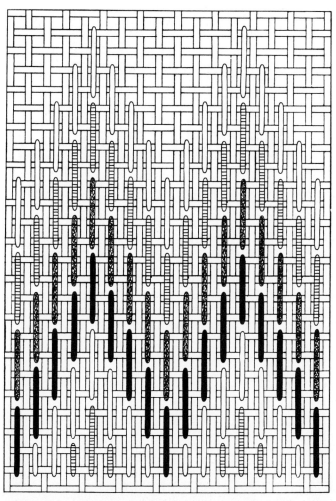

FLOWER

The sample is worked on Zweigart® Congress cloth with Anchor® floss.

This stitch is worked in blocks of 4 stitches across the row.

Starting 3 vertical threads from the left-hand corner and 1 horizontal thread down at **1**, work a vertical straight stitch over 2 horizontal canvas threads (**1-2**). Then work 2 vertical straight stitches over 4 horizontal canvas threads (**3-4, 5-6**). End the block by working another vertical straight stitch like the first over 2 horizontal canvas threads (**7-8**). This completes the first block.

Skip 2 vertical canvas threads and work another block as the first (**9-10, 11-12,** etc.). Repeat to the end of the row. These are represented as solid black stitches in Diagram A.

The second row is worked below the first, starting 3 horizontal threads and 1 vertical thread from the upper left-hand corner at **A**. Work this row of blocks with horizontal straight stitches over 2, over 4, over 4, and over 2 vertical canvas threads (**A-B, C-D, E-F, G-H**).

These are the shaded stitches in Diagram A.

When the straight stitches are completed, insert a cross-stitch over the intersection of 2 vertical and 2 horizontal canvas threads left unworked between the blocks of vertical straight stitches and a small cross-stitch over the intersection of 1 vertical and 1 horizontal canvas thread left unworked between the blocks of horizontal straight stitches. These are the white stitches on Diagram A.

The cross-stitches may be worked in the same or a contrasting color.

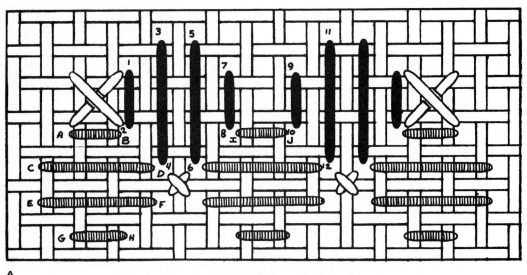

A

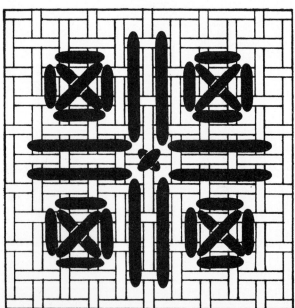

B

FLY
(open loop stitch, y-stitch)

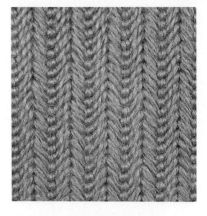

The sample is worked on #12 Zweigart® Mono canvas with DMC® Floralia® (3-ply Persian yarn).

The Fly stitch is worked in vertical rows.

To work, start with a small straight stitch (**1-2**). Next, make a loop over 2 vertical canvas threads and tie it with a small straight stitch (**5-6**). Start the third part of the stitch at **7** and continue as shown in the diagram.

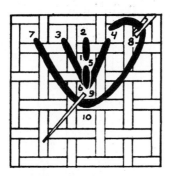

FOUR, THREE, TWO CROSS

The sample is worked on #12 Zweigart® Mono canvas with Anchor® Tapisserie (tapestry yarn).

This stitch is worked over 4 horizontal and 4 vertical canvas threads, forming a pattern of squares across the row.

Start with a vertical straight stitch over 4 horizontal canvas threads (**1-2**). Then place the second stitch over 3 horizontal canvas threads (**3-4**) and the third over 2 horizontal canvas threads (**5-6**), forming the left side of the stitch.

Next place 3 horizontal straight stitches over 2, 3, and 4 vertical canvas threads (**7-8, 9-10, 11-12**) at right angles to the first set of stitches. This will form the right side of the stitch.

Finally, place a diagonal stitch from the top right corner of the stitch to the bottom left corner (**13-14**).

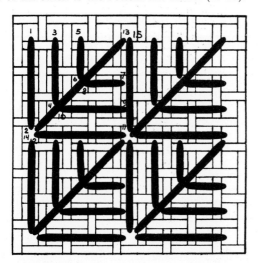

FRAME

The sample is worked on #14 Zweigart® Mono canvas with DMC® Floralia® (3-ply Persian yarn).

This stitch forms a frame around a central rectangle. Place the darkest shades at the center and the lightest on the perimeter.

Begin stitching with the lightest shade or color, forming the outer frame (**1-2, 3-4, 5-6, 7-8**).

Change to the next lightest color or shade and continue to work the frame in an inward direction (**9-10, 11-12, 13-14, 15-16**). The frame is continued using the medium color or shade (**17-18, 19-20, 21-22, 23-24**).

Finish by working the darkest color or shade in the center of the frame (**25-26, 27-28**).

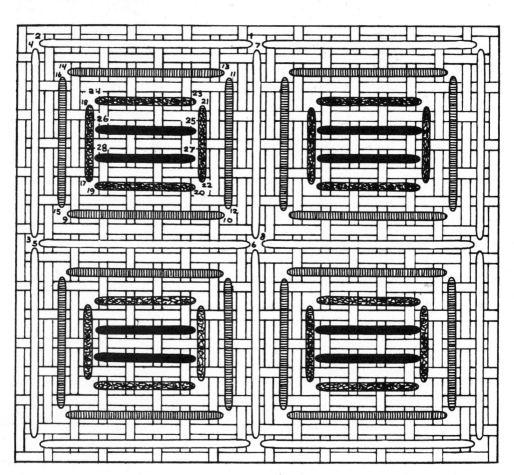

FRENCH 1

The sample is worked on #12 Zweigart® Mono canvas with DMC® Floralia® (3-ply Persian yarn).

First, work a vertical straight stitch over 4 horizontal canvas threads (**1-2**). Now take a small horizontal stitch over this stitch and the vertical canvas thread to the left (**3-4**). Return to the starting hole and place another vertical straight stitch next to the first (**5-6**). Make a small horizontal stitch over this stitch and the vertical canvas thread to the right (**7-8**).

Work horizontally across the row, starting the second row 2 horizontal canvas threads down and 1 vertical canvas thread to the right.

FRENCH 2
(double tie-down, Paris)

The sample is worked on #12 Zweigart® Mono canvas with Anchor® floss.

This stitch is composed of 2 elongated upright crosses sharing the same hole.

Start with an upright stitch worked over 4 horizontal canvas threads (**1-2**). Work a small backstitch (**3-4**) in the center over the upright stitch and the vertical canvas thread directly to the left of this stitch. Work the second upright stitch over the same 4 canvas threads right next to and in the same hole as the first stitch (**5-6**). The tie backstitch is placed across the vertical canvas thread to the right of this stitch and the upright stitch just made (**7-8**). Notice that both tie backstitches are worked from the outside of the stitch to the center.

Work the French stitch in diagonal rows.

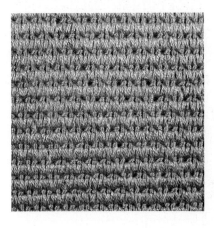

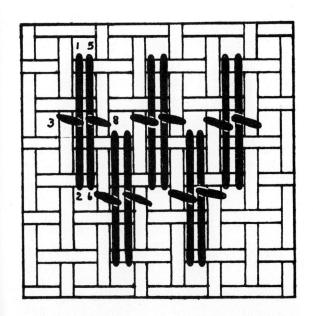

FRENCH, DIAGONAL

The sample is worked on #10 Zweigart® Mono canvas with Anchor® Tapisserie (tapestry yarn).

This stitch is worked as an elongated upright cross and is only a distant relative to the French stitch.

First, from the bottom up, make a diagonal row of upright stitches working over 4 and back under 2 horizontal canvas threads (**1-2, 3-4, 5-6,** etc.). See Diagram A.

Next work the tie stitches at the center of each stitch over 2 horizontal canvas threads (**A-B, C-D, E-F,** etc.). Diagram B shows the placement of the next rows.

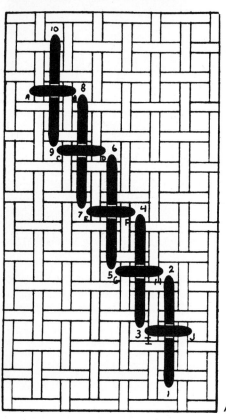

A

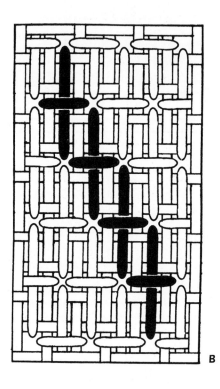

B

FRENCH KNOT
(French dot, knotted, wound)

The sample is worked on #18 Zweigart® Mono canvas with DMC® Floralia® (2-ply Persian yarn).

The French Knot may be worked as a solid textured area or individually where dots or knots are needed.

The weight or ply of the thread or yarn will determine the size of the finished knot. *Do not wind the yarn around the needle more times to make a larger knot.*

The French Knot is worked over the intersection of 1 vertical and 1 horizontal canvas thread.

To work, bring the needle to the front of the canvas in the spot you want the knot (**A**). Hold it firmly and twist the yarn *once* around the needle. Turn the point of the needle clockwise (see diagram) and insert it over the intersection at **B**.

The sample was worked using 2-ply Persian yarn on #18 canvas, stitching in a Basketweave (Tent) pattern (page 144) in every other hole and every other row. (See Diagram B.)

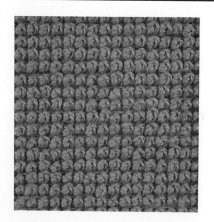

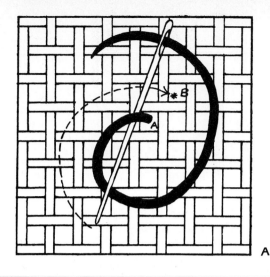

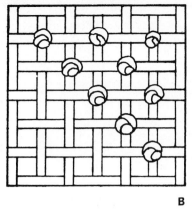

B

A

FRENCH KNOT WITH TAIL
(French knot on stalks, Italian knot, long-tail French knot, long tack knot, stamen knot)

The sample is worked on #18 Zweigart® Mono canvas with DMC® #5 perle cotton.

This variation of the French Knot is made with a tail extending from the knot.

Start by working a diagonal stitch for the tail (**1-2**). See Diagram A. Bring the yarn back to the front at **3**.

Work the French Knot over the intersection of 1 vertical and 1 horizontal canvas thread. See Diagram B.

Diagram C shows a placement of these stitches worked as stamens for a flower.

A 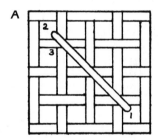   **B**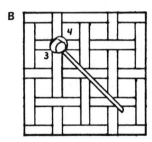

C

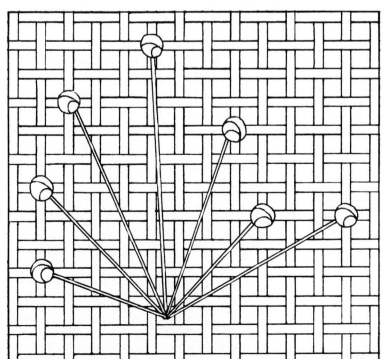

G

GINGHAM

The sample is worked on #12 Zweigart® Mono canvas with DMC® Floralia® (3-ply Persian yarn).

The Gingham stitch is made of blocks of 4 vertical and horizontal stitches in 3 color shades, which resembles gingham cloth.

Working horizontally across the row, start with the darkest color and stitch a block of 4 vertical straight stitches over 3 horizontal canvas threads (**1-2, 3-4, 5-6, 7-8**). Skip 4 vertical canvas threads and repeat the block (**9-10,** etc.) across the row.

Change to the medium shade and work blocks of 4 horizontal straight stitches in the spaces left (**A-B, C-D, E-F, G-H,** etc.) across the row.

Start Row 2 using the medium shade, working 4 horizontal straight stitches over 4 vertical canvas threads. Skip 3 vertical canvas threads and repeat the block across the row.

Finish by working 4 vertical straight stitches in the spaces left (**a-b, c-d, e-f, g-h,** etc.).

Repeat these 2 rows for the pattern.

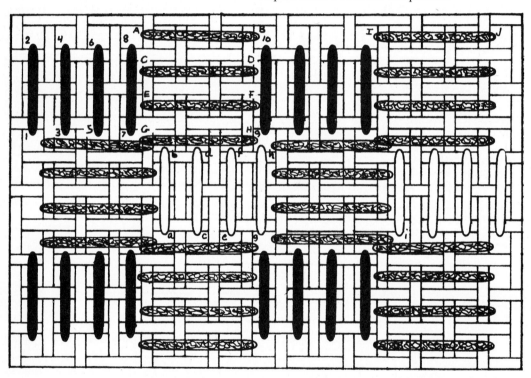

GINGHAM MOSAIC

The sample is worked on #14 Zweigart® Mono canvas with DMC® Floralia® (3-ply Persian yarn).

The Gingham Mosaic is worked entirely in Mosaic stitches (page 104), changing colors to create the gingham pattern.

Work horizontally across the row, skipping 2 vertical canvas threads between the Mosaic blocks (**1-2, 3-4, 5-6, 7-8,** etc.), starting with the medium shade.

Fill in the spaces with a Mosaic stitch, using the darkest shade (**A-B, C-D, E-F,** etc.).

Row 2 is worked exactly the same, alternating the white and the medium shade across the row.

Repeat these 2 rows for the pattern.

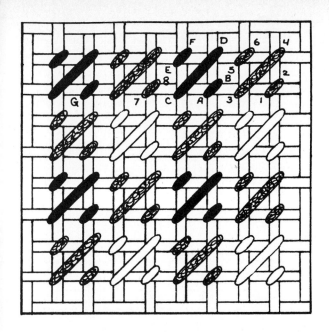

GINGHAM SCOTCH

The sample is worked on #14 Zweigart® Mono canvas with DMC® Floralia® (3-ply Persian yarn).

The Gingham Scotch stitch alternates blocks of Scotch stitch (page 130) in 2 colors across each row.

Start by stitching the Scotch stitch blocks in the medium shade over 3 vertical and 3 horizontal canvas threads (**1-2, 3-4, 5-6, 7-8, 9-10**), skipping 3 vertical canvas threads between the blocks across the row.

Next, work Scotch stitch blocks in the spaces left, using the darkest shade (**A-B, C-D, E-F, G-H, I-J,** etc.).

Row 2 is worked exactly the same, alternating the white and the medium shade across the row.

Repeat these 2 rows for the pattern.

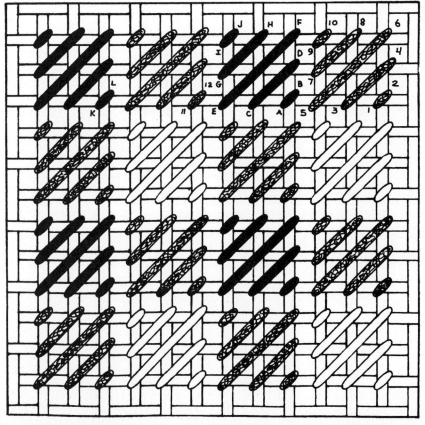

GOBELIN, CROSSED
(crossed straight)

The sample is worked on #10 Zweigart® Mono canvas with DMC® Floralia® (3-ply Persian yarn).

The Crossed Gobelin stitch is worked over 6 horizontal and 2 vertical canvas threads.

First work the Upright Gobelin stitch over 6 horizontal canvas threads (**1-2**). Then place the cross-stitch over the center 2 horizontal and 2 vertical canvas threads (**3-4, 5-6**). Leave 1 space (2 vertical canvas threads) between stitches and continue across the row.

The second row is fitted into the spaces left between the stitches of the first row. See diagram.

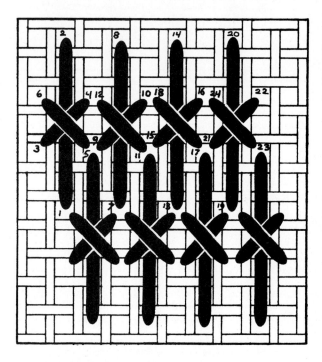

GOBELIN, ENCROACHING

The sample is worked on #12 Zweigart® Mono canvas with DMC® Floralia® (3-ply Persian yarn).

This stitch works up quickly and creates a smooth surface on the front and a thick padding on the reverse side of the canvas. It is worked in rows with individual stitches encroaching into the spaces between the stitches of the previous row.

Each stitch is worked over 1 vertical and 2 or more horizontal canvas threads. (See diagram for stitch placement).

GOBELIN, INTERLOCKING

The sample is worked on #10 Zweigart® Mono canvas with DMC® Floralia® (3-ply Persian yarn).

The Interlocking Gobelin stitch can be worked over 2–5 horizontal canvas threads. The first row is worked exactly like the Upright Gobelin. The next rows are also worked over 3 horizontal canvas threads, but they use only 2 new horizontal canvas threads and overlap 1 thread of the previous row, sharing the hole. Always place the new stitch to the left of the stitch of the previous row. (See diagram).

This is a fast-working background stitch.

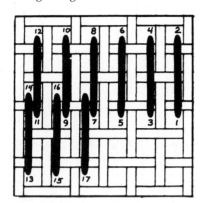

GOBELIN, SLANTING 1

The sample is worked on #10 Zweigart® Mono canvas with DMC® Floralia® (3-ply Persian yarn).

The Slanting Gobelin stitch is one of the easiest slanting stitches. It is worked over 1 vertical canvas thread and 2–5 horizontal canvas threads from left to right across the row. Work this stitch on a frame to avoid the canvas distortion common with all slanting stitches. (See diagram.)

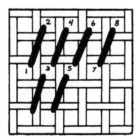

GOBELIN, SLANTING 2
(oblique Gobelin, diagonal)

The sample is worked on #10 Zweigart® Mono canvas with Anchor® Tapisserie (tapestry yarn).

This Slanting Gobelin stitch is worked in rows over 2–5 horizontal and 1–3 vertical canvas threads. It is generally used as a border, framing, or background stitch.

This stitch will distort the canvas and leave holes between the rows if your tension is too tight. Working on a frame is recommended.

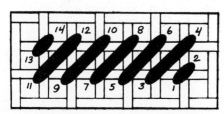

GOBELIN, SPLIT

The sample is worked on #12 Zweigart® Mono canvas with DMC® Floralia® (3-ply Persian yarn).

The Split Gobelin stitch is used for background or for detail areas. It is one of the few canvas stitches that can be worked in subtle tones for shading.

The first row is worked over 3 horizontal canvas threads exactly like the Upright Gobelin. The next rows are also worked over 3 horizontal canvas threads, but they use only 2 *new* horizontal canvas threads and encroach over 1 horizontal canvas thread of the previous row, splitting the yarn of the previous stitch.

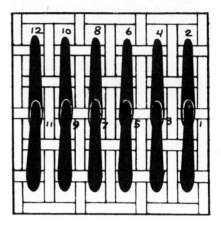

GOBELIN, TRAME

The sample is worked on #12 Zweigart® Mono canvas with DMC® Floralia® (3-ply Persian yarn).

The Gobelin Tramé stitch is a combination of an Upright Gobelin worked over a length of yarn laid (tramé) over an indefinite number of vertical canvas threads, producing the look of woven fabric.

First, come up from the back at **A**, gently lay the yarn over the chosen number of vertical canvas threads, and return down at the end of the row at **B**. Come back up under 2 horizontal canvas threads at **C**. Let this yarn stay on the right side while you work a row of Gobelin stitches over the tramé yarn and 2 horizontal canvas threads in a lighter shade of the same color or a different color yarn (**1-2, 3-4, 5-6**, etc.). Lay the tramé yarn 1 row ahead of the Gobelin stitches to avoid twisting or coiling the yarn. The second row is worked from right to left.

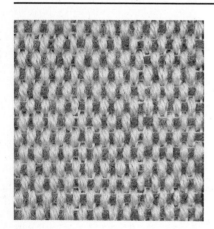

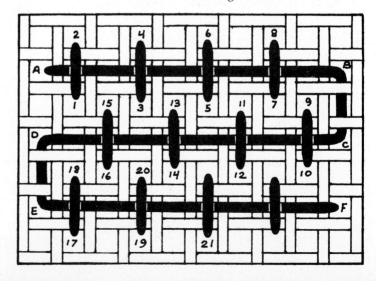

GOBELIN, UPRIGHT
(Gobelin droit, straight Gobelin, satin, upright)

The sample is worked on #12 Zweigart® Mono canvas with DMC® Floralia® (3-ply Persian yarn).

The Upright Gobelin stitch is the basic Gobelin stitch and can be worked over 2–5 horizontal canvas threads. It is also the primary Bargello stitch (see "Bargello," page 16).

Be careful to keep your tension relaxed and avoid twisting the yarn.

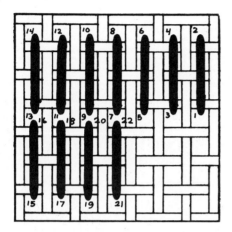

GROUNDING, SMALL

The sample is worked on #12 Zweigart® Mono canvas with Anchor® Tapisserie (tapestry yarn).

The Grounding, Small stitch is used for background and for filling large areas of canvas.

First, work a cross-stitch over 4 horizontal and 4 vertical canvas threads (1-2, 3-4). Then, work a long diagonal stitch over 3 horizontal and 1 vertical canvas threads (5-6), point left.

Next, work a long diagonal stitch from the center hole at the bottom of the cross to the top of the cross, 1 space below the start of the cross at 1 (7-8). Repeat for the other side (9-10, 11-12).

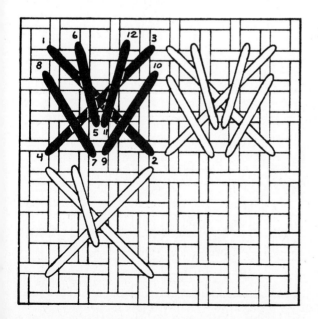

H

HERRINGBONE
(plaited Gobelin)

The sample is worked on #12 Zweigart® Mono canvas with DMC® Floralia® (3-ply Persian yarn).

The Herringbone is a woven linear-type stitch that *must* be worked from left to right on each row. *The canvas is never turned.*

It is worked over 4 horizontal and 4 vertical canvas threads and back under 2 vertical canvas threads (see diagram). The next row is started 2 horizontal canvas threads below the first row.

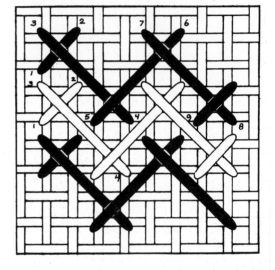

HERRINGBONE, DOUBLE INTERLACED

The sample is worked on #12 Zweigart® Mono canvas with DMC® Floralia® (3-ply Persian yarn) and Anchor® floss.

This stitch is a combination of the double herringbone and an interlacing woven in a path as marked in the diagram.

Note that in working the double herringbone, some stitches are worked *under* instead of over the preceding stitch. Follow the diagram carefully.

HILTON AMADEUS
(amadeus)

The sample is worked on #18 Zweigart® Mono canvas with DMC® #3 perle cotton.

Jean Hilton is credited with originating many new and unusual stitches. I have included three of my favorites in this dictionary. If you want to try other Hilton stitches or variations of these stitches, see "Selected Bibliography," page 193.

The Hilton Amadeus was developed in 1985. Follow the diagram exactly, starting with a central common stem (**1-2**) and working each half independently. The second half shares the same stem holes with the first half.

Come up at **3** and down at **4**, going *over* the **1-2** stitch. Continue in this manner until the first half is completed, then go back to **1** and continue for the other side.

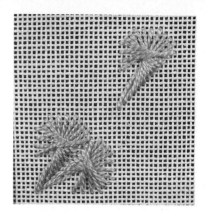

			14		12		10		8									
		16								6								
	18									4								
	20										2							
	22											25		2				
											23				4			
	24								21							6		
								19									8	
	26						17											
						15											10	
					13													
				11													12	
			9															
			7														14	
		5													16			
	3													18				
	1						26		24		22		20					

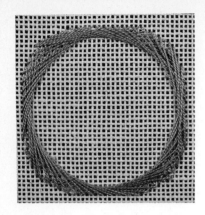

HILTON JESSICA
(Jessica)

The sample is worked on #18 Zweigart® Mono canvas with DMC® #5 perle cotton.

Jean Hilton developed this stitch in the 1980s. Many variations are charted in her book *Needlepoint Stitches* (see "Selected Bibliography," page 193.)

Follow the diagram, remembering that you must have 2 stitches in every hole. From **99** to **100** and **119** to **120**, slip the needle *under* the previously worked stitches and into the correct hole.

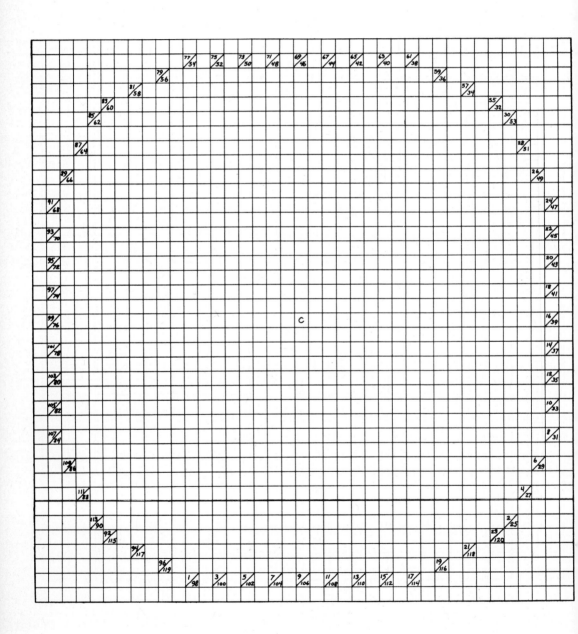

HILTON MISTAKE
(mistake)

The sample is worked on #18 Zweigart® Mono canvas with DMC® #3 perle cotton.

The Hilton Mistake stitch was developed by Jean Hilton in the 1970s when a student of hers was trying unsuccessfully to do a Waffle stitch.

It is a difficult stitch to master but well worth the effort. Count carefully when you start (**1-2, 3-4, 5-6, 7-8**). Each stitch is laid over the previous stitches. Continue, following the diagram exactly.

Use a firm but relaxed tension to avoid distortion.

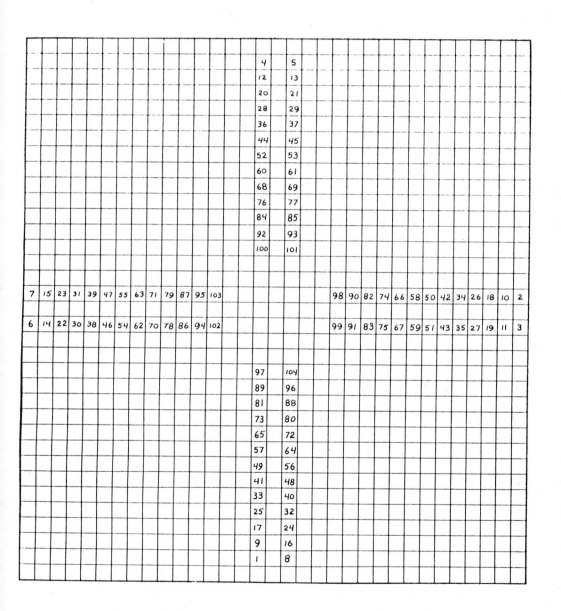

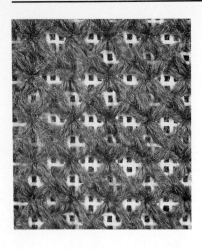

HOUNDSTOOTH
(hound's tooth)

The sample is worked on #12 Zweigart® Mono canvas with DMC® Floralia® (3-ply Persian yarn).

This stitch can be worked over 3, 4, 5, or 6 canvas threads. The sample is worked over 4 horizontal and 4 vertical canvas threads.

First, make a diagonal stitch over 4 horizontal and 4 vertical canvas threads (**1-2**). Bring the needle up at the top left-hand corner (**3**), looping the yarn under and then over the diagonal stitch, coming back down in the same hole (**4**).

Next, bring the needle up at the lower right-hand corner (**5-6**) of the square. Loop the yarn over the diagonal stitch, through the loop previously formed and back down into the same hole (**5-6**). Continue across the row.

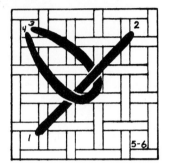

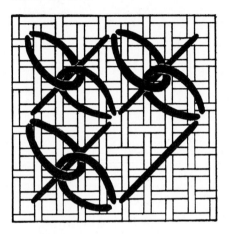

HUNGARIAN

The sample is worked on #10 Zweigart® Mono canvas with DMC® Floralia® (3-ply Persian yarn).

The Hungarian stitch consists of 3 vertical stitches that form a diamond shape.

The pattern is formed by skipping a space between each stitch unit. When it is worked in 2 colors, a diagonal checkerboard pattern is created.

This stitch is very similar to the Parisian stitch (page 111).

First, work a vertical stitch over 2 horizontal canvas threads (**1-2**). Then, work a longer vertical stitch over 4 horizontal canvas threads (**3-4**), and finally the last stitch over 2 horizontal canvas threads. Skip 2 canvas threads between the stitch units. The second row is worked between the stitches of the first row with the longer vertical stitch encroaching 2 horizontal threads into the first row. (See diagram.)

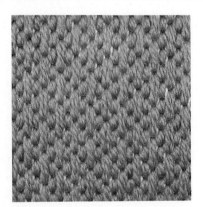

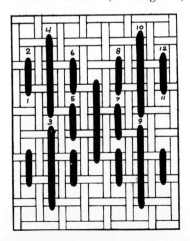

HUNGARIAN, DOUBLE

The sample is worked on #12 Zweigart® Mono canvas with DMC® Floralia® (3-ply Persian yarn).

This variation of the Hungarian stitch places a second vertical straight stitch next to each original stitch, forming a horizontally elongated stitch as shown in the diagram.

The second row is worked in a contrasting color.

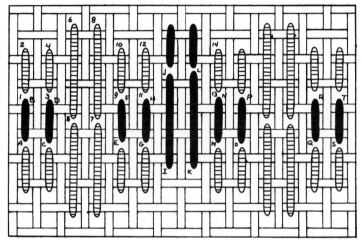

HUNGARIAN, GROUNDING 1

The sample is worked on #10 Zweigart® Mono canvas with DMC® Floralia® (3-ply Persian yarn).

This stitch is often mistaken for Florentine or Bargello stitches.

It may be worked over a varying number of horizontal canvas threads. In the sample (see diagram), the vertical straight stitches are worked in a horizontal row over 4 horizontal canvas threads (**1-2, 3-4, 5-6,** etc.). Then work the filling stitches (**a-b, c-d, e-f,** etc.) in another shade of the same color or a contrasting color.

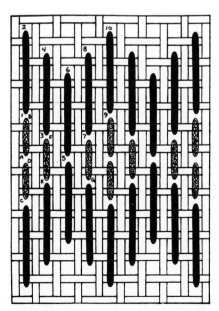

85

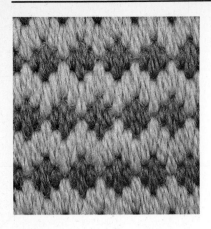

HUNGARIAN, GROUNDING 2

The sample is worked on #12 Zweigart® Mono canvas with DMC® Floralia® (3-ply Persian yarn).

Work as for Grounding 1 Hungarian, following the diagram.

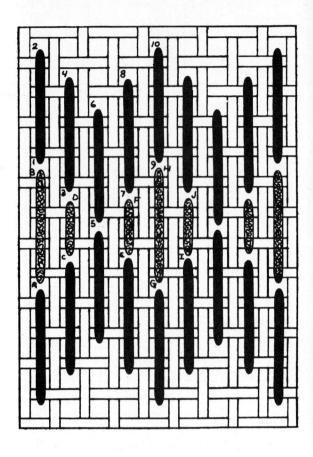

HUNGARIAN, HORIZONTAL

The sample is worked on #10 Zweigart® Mono canvas with Anchor® Tapisserie (tapestry yarn).

This is a Hungarian stitch turned horizontally and worked in blocks of 3 stitches in a vertical row (**1-2, 3-4, 5-6, 7-8,** etc.).

It may be worked in 1 or 2 colors.

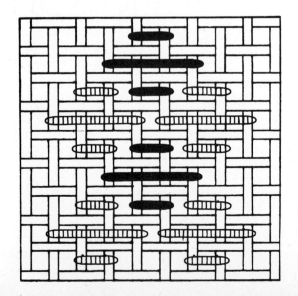

INTERWOVEN CROSS
(interlaced cross, woven cross)

The sample is worked on #12 Zweigart® Mono canvas with Anchor® Tapisserie (tapestry yarn).

The Interwoven Cross is a squared stitch made of 6 diagonal stitches. It is worked over 4 horizontal and 4 vertical canvas threads.

First, make a basic cross-stitch (**1-2, 3-4**). Then, following the diagram, add **5-6, 7-8,** and **9-10**. The last stitch, **11-12**, is worked taking the thread *over* the 2 stitches (**3-4** and **9-10**) and slipped *under* the last stitch (**5-6**).

The interwoven stitch can be used as a single accent stitch or worked in rows to cover large areas.

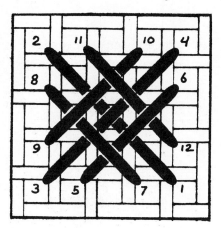

ITALIAN CROSS
(Italian, two-sided)

The sample is worked on #12 Zweigart® Mono canvas with Anchor® Tapisserie (tapestry yarn).

The Italian Cross is a cross inside a square of upright stitches and can be worked over 3 or 4 horizontal and 3 or 4 vertical canvas threads. (See Diagram A.)

First, work the cross-stitch (**1-2, 3-4**). Then, work the left-side upright stitch (**5-6**), and, last, the bottom (**7-8**). (See Diagram B.)

This stitch works well as a border or a background.

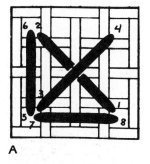

A

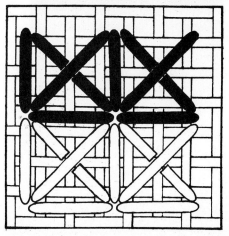

B

J

JACQUARD

The sample is worked on #10 Zweigart® Mono canvas with Anchor® Tapisserie (tapestry yarn).

The Jacquard stitch is a combination of the Byzantine (page 36) and tent stitches. It is worked in stepped rows of 5–6 diagonal slanting stitches over 2 horizontal and 2 vertical canvas threads. The same number of tent stitches are then placed on either side of these diagonal stitches.

This stitch may be worked in 1 or 2 colors and should be worked on a frame to avoid canvas distortion.

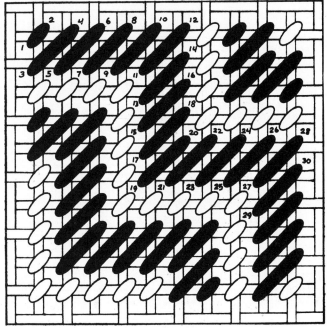

K

KALEM
(knitting Gobelin, knitting)

The sample is worked on #12 Zweigart® Mono canvas with Anchor® Tapisserie (tapestry yarn).

The Kalem stitch resembles hand knitting more than any other stitch. It is worked in vertical rows over 1 vertical and 2 horizontal canvas threads.

Start at the top and work in a downward direction for the first half of the stitch (1-2, 3-4, 5-6) and from the bottom upward for the second half (7-8, 9-10, 11-12). (See diagram.)

KNITTED

The sample is worked on #12 Zweigart® Mono canvas with Anchor® Tapisserie (tapestry yarn).

The Knitted stitch closely resembles the Kalem stitch, but is worked over 2 horizontal and 2 vertical canvas threads, producing a wider, less inclined stitch.

It is worked in vertical rows starting at the top in a downward direction for the first half of the stitch (**1-2, 3-4, 5-6,** etc.) and from the bottom in an upward direction for the second half.

L

LAZY ROMAN II

The sample is worked on #10 Zweigart® Mono canvas with Anchor® Tapisserie (tapestry yarn).

This stitch is a variation of the Roman II (page 126) stitch. Placed on the horizontal, it is worked in staggered vertical rows.

Start by working a horizontal straight stitch over 4 vertical canvas threads (**1-2**). Place another straight stitch below it (**3-4**). Then work the third stitch a half-step down and to the right (**5-6**), and the fourth directly beneath it (**7-8**).

The next block is worked a half-step to the left below the first block (**9-10, 11-12**).

Place the vertical straight stitches over 3 horizontal canvas threads *after* the blocks are completed. They may be worked in the same or a second color.

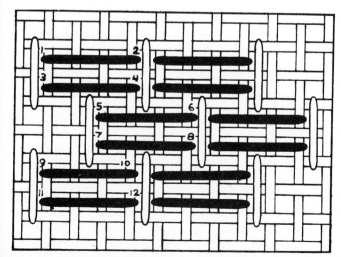

LEAF 1

The sample is worked on #14 Zweigart® Mono canvas with DMC® Floralia® (3-ply Persian yarn).

This is the basic, most-used stitch of this kind and is recognized as *the* leaf stitch. It can be worked in horizontal rows or on the diagonal in 1 or more colors.

Follow the numbering on the diagram exactly. A vein can be added (see Leaf 3, opposite) for added interest and texture.

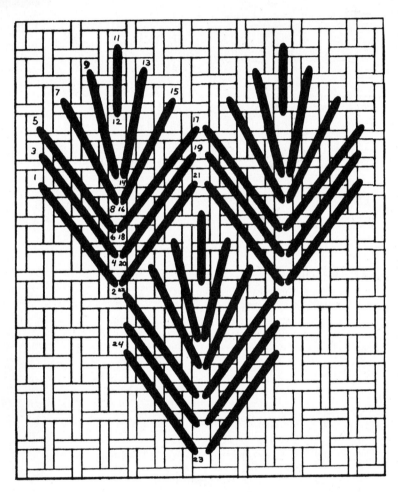

LEAF 2

The sample is worked on #14 Zweigart® Mono canvas with DMC® Floralia® (3-ply Persian yarn).

This variation of the leaf stitch can be worked on the diagonal or in horizontal rows.

An interesting diagonal stripe pattern is made by using different colors for each row.

Follow the numbering on the diagram exactly.

LEAF 3

The sample is worked on #14 Zweigart® Mono canvas with DMC® Floralia® (3-ply Persian yarn).

This is a variation of the leaf stitch with a vein placed to add interest and cover the exposed canvas. It can be worked in a second color for more emphasis.

The pattern works well as a four-way medallion (see Leaf, Medallion, page 94).

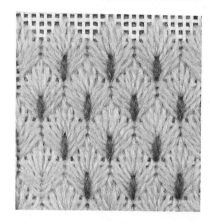

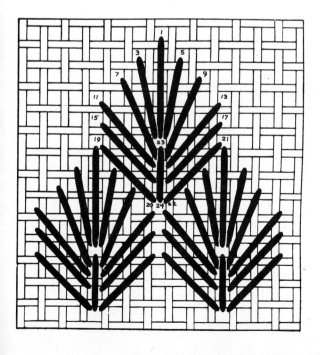

LEAF, CRETAN

The sample is worked on #10 Zweigart® Mono canvas with DMC® Floralia® (3-ply Persian yarn).

This variation of the leaf stitch forms a braid down the center of the leaf shape. It is usually used alone as a surface ornamental stitch.

Follow the numbering on the diagram exactly.

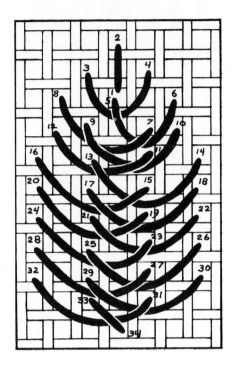

LEAF 1, DIAGONAL

The sample is worked on #10 Zweigart® Mono canvas with DMC® Floralia® (3-ply Persian yarn).

This variation of the leaf stitch slants to the upper left and is worked on the diagonal.

As with the other leaf stitches, it is important to follow the numbering on the diagram exactly.

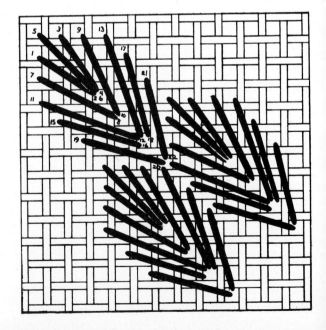

LEAF 2, DIAGONAL

The sample is worked on #10 Zweigart® Mono canvas with DMC® Floralia® (3-ply Persian yarn).

This variation of the diagonal leaf stitch has a stem covering the exposed canvas threads worked in the same color. Work the leaves on the diagonal in 1 color for an allover pattern or in 2 colors for a stripe.

Follow the numbering on the diagram carefully.

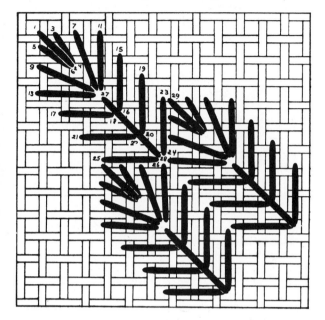

LEAF, DIAMOND
(fan leaf, ray leaf)

The sample is worked on #14 Zweigart® Mono canvas with DMC® Floralia® (3-ply Persian yarn).

This variation of the leaf stitch forms the shape of a diamond. It is worked on the diagonal.

The pattern can be made in 1 color or in 2 alternating colors to form a diagonal stripe.

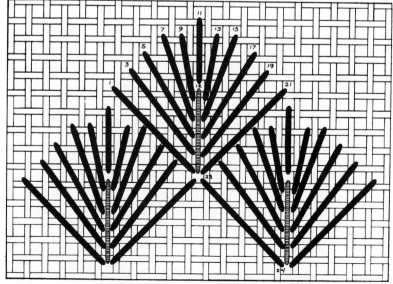

LEAF, HERRINGBONE
(close herringbone)

The sample is worked on #10 Zweigart® Mono canvas with DMC® Floralia® (3-ply Persian yarn).

This is a variation of the leaf stitch in shape only. It produces an interesting surface ornamental motif.

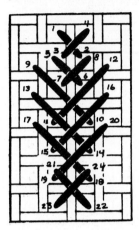

LEAF, MEDALLION
(four-way leaf)

The sample is worked on Zweigart® Congress cloth with Anchor® floss.

This is worked as a single ornamental motif with tent stitches filling around it as a background.

Start at **1** and work the diagonal stitches as shown in the diagram in a clockwise direction to form the 4 leaves.

The vein stitches are worked in after the medallion is complete, in the same or a contrasting color.

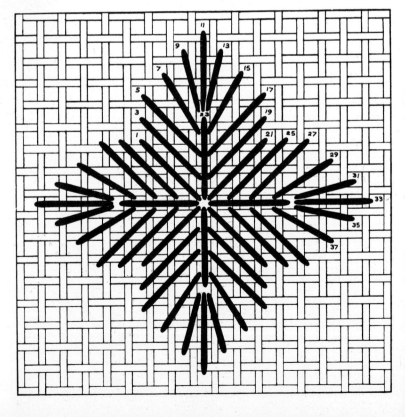

LEAF, RAISED CLOSE HERRINGBONE

The sample is worked on #10 Zweigart® Mono canvas with Anchor® Tapisserie (tapestry yarn).

This leaf stitch variation is worked alone as an accent or ornamental motif on the *surface* of the work. The stitch appears to be three-dimensional.

To start, make a small vertical straight stitch over 1 horizontal canvas thread (**1-2**). *All the other stitches are looped through this stitch.*

Next, bring the needle to the front at **3**, loop through the vertical straight stitch (**1-2**), and return at **4**.

Follow this method until all the loops are worked (**5-6, 7-8, 9-10, 11-12,** and **13-14**).

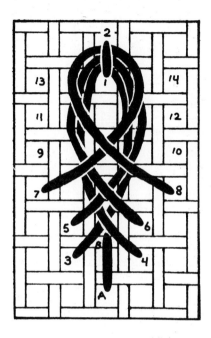

LEAF, ROUMANIAN

The sample is worked on #12 Zweigart® Mono canvas with DMC® Floralia® (3-ply Persian yarn).

The Roumanian leaf is worked like a Fly stitch (page 69), but shaped like a leaf. It can be worked horizontally, or vertically as shown in the diagram.

Follow the numbering on the diagram carefully.

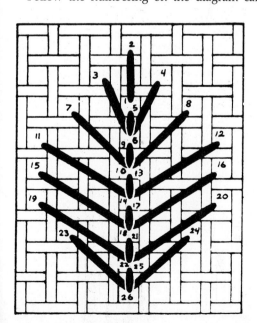

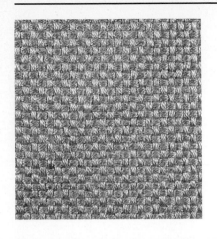

LINEN
(cloth)

The sample is worked on #14 Zweigart® Mono canvas with Anchor® floss.

This stitch forms a woven surface that resembles fabric. It is a good background stitch for covering large areas.

Work the rows diagonally from the top right corner to the lower left and then back vertically from the lower left to the upper right, following the numbers as diagramed. Note that each stitch is worked over 2 canvas threads.

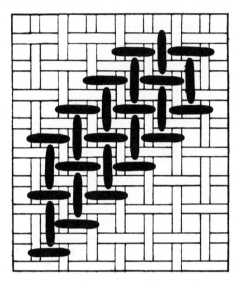

LINK, SURFACE

The sample is worked on #12 Zweigart® Mono canvas with DMC® Floralia® (3-ply Persian yarn).

The Surface Link stitch makes a good filling stitch and can also be used as an ornamental or decorative motif when worked over a tent-stitched area (or even on a fabric or sweater).

First, make a vertical straight stitch over 4 horizontal canvas threads (**1-2**). Then, bring the needle to the front 1 vertical canvas thread to the right of the top of the stitch (**3**).

Slip the needle under the vertical straight stitch, looping the yarn under and over it before inserting the needle 1 vertical canvas thread to the right of the bottom of the first stitch (**4**).

This stitch can be worked across the row or on the diagonal.

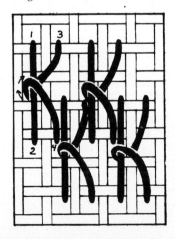

LINKED, STEPPED
(linked, half-drop)

The sample is worked on #12 Zweigart® Mono canvas with Anchor® Tapisserie (tapestry yarn).

This stitch can be made over any *even* number of horizontal canvas threads with 4 or more upright stitches (**1-2, 3-4, 5-6, 7-8**) and 1 straight horizontal stitch (**9-10**) worked over the center to tie them together.

The Stepped Linked stitch is worked on the diagonal with each unit of stitches started at the middle of the previous stitch (see diagram).

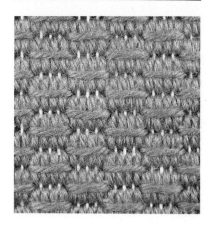

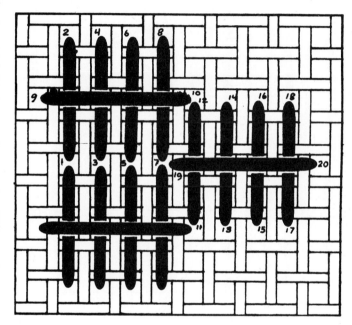

LONG-ARMED CROSS
(double back, Greek, long-legged cross)

The sample is worked on #14 Zweigart® Mono canvas with Anchor® Tapisserie (tapestry yarn).

This stitch is worked in rows and resembles an interwoven braid.

Start with a cross-stitch over 2 horizontal and 2 vertical canvas threads (**1-2, 3-4**). Come up from the back in the same hole as the first stitch and go over 2 horizontal and 4 vertical canvas threads to make the long arm (**5-6**). Next, go under 2 horizontal canvas threads, coming up at **7** and down at **8**. Repeat from the long arm (**9**) across the row as shown in the diagram. Rotate the canvas for the return row.

This stitch works up easily once a rhythm is established.

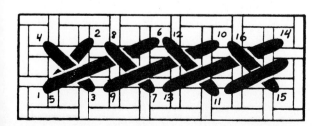

LOZENGE SATIN
(satin lozenge)

The sample is worked on #14 Zweigart® Mono canvas with DMC® Floralia® (3-ply Persian yarn).

The Lozenge Satin stitch is used for filling large areas or backgrounds. The pattern is made by placing long vertical satin stitches as shown on the diagram.

Work in horizontal rows beginning at the left-hand side (**1-2, 3-4, 5-6,** etc.). After the left-side right triangle is finished, work the center groups of 3 stitches. Finally, complete the right-side right triangle.

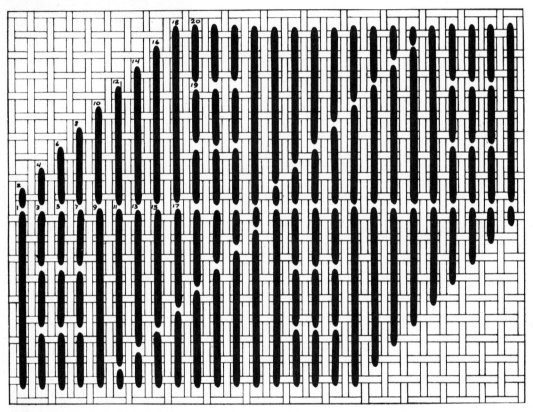

M

MALTESE CROSS
(interlacing)

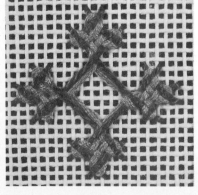

The sample is worked on #12 Zweigart® Mono canvas with Anchor® Tapisserie (tapestry yarn) and Anchor® floss.

The Maltese Cross is worked on a base of the Double Hungarian (page 85) stitch (see Diagram A). Follow the numbering on the diagram *exactly*.

Next, using a lighter color yarn, come up from the back at **A** and weave through the foundation stitches following the direction of the arrows. End at **B**.

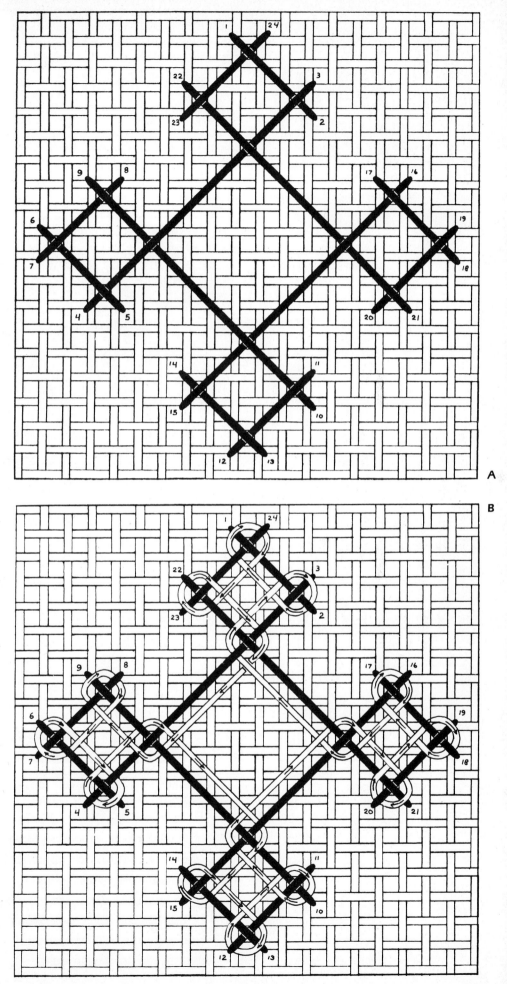

MILANESE

The sample is worked on #14 Zweigart® Mono canvas with Anchor® Tapisserie (tapestry yarn).

The Milanese stitch is a diagonal stitch worked in rows from the top left to the bottom right. It resembles a row of triangles or arrowheads with the first row pointing in an upward direction and the next in a downward direction, interlocking with each other.

Each unit of 4 stitches is worked over 1, 2, 3, and, finally, 4 horizontal and vertical canvas threads as shown in the diagram.

This stitch can be worked in 1 color as a background or 2 colors to form an alternating stripe pattern.

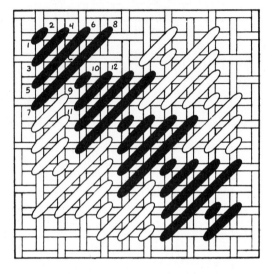

MILANESE, STRAIGHT

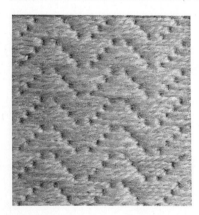

The sample is worked on #12 Zweigart® Mono canvas with DMC® Floralia® (3-ply Persian yarn).

The Straight Milanese stitch is a variation of the Milanese stitch.

Each triangle is formed by working 5 straight horizontal stitches over 2, 4, 6, and 8 vertical canvas threads.

These triangle units are then worked in a vertical row from the top in a downward direction. The next row is worked from the bottom in an upward direction, reversing the direction of the triangles (see diagram).

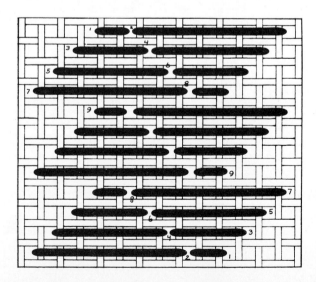

MILANESE PINWHEEL
(pinwheel)

The sample is worked on Zweigart® Congress cloth with Anchor® floss.

This large variation of the Milanese stitch is usually used as an individual motif or accent stitch. It can also be worked as an allover pattern.

The stitch is made by working the units of the Milanese stitch triangles around a center hole, beginning with the tent stitch marked **A**. Continue working the slanted stitches until the triangle is complete (8 stitches). Work each triangle in a counterclockwise direction until all 8 units are complete. (See diagram.)

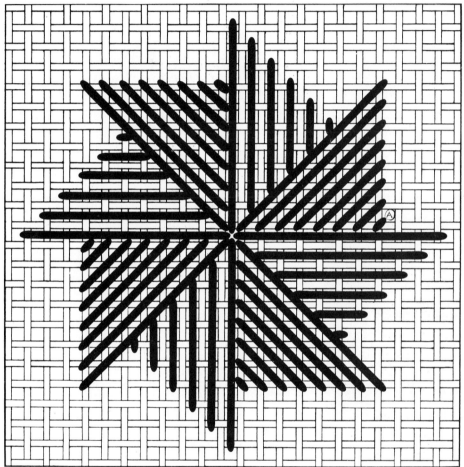

MILANESE VARIATION

The sample is worked on #12 Zweigart® Mono canvas with DMC® Floralia® (3-ply Persian yarn).

This is a combination stitch with Milanese straight stitches alternating with triangle-shaped Eye stitches (page 63).

Work a triangle eye stitch from left to right by working 11 stitches over 6 horizontal canvas threads into a center hole (**1-AA, 2-AA, 3-AA, 4-AA,** etc.).

Next, make a straight Milanese stitch by working 6 graduating horizontal straight stitches over 2, 4, 6, 8, 10, and 12 vertical canvas threads (**A-B, C-D, E-F,** etc.).

This stitch is worked in 2 different-weight yarns in 2 different colors.

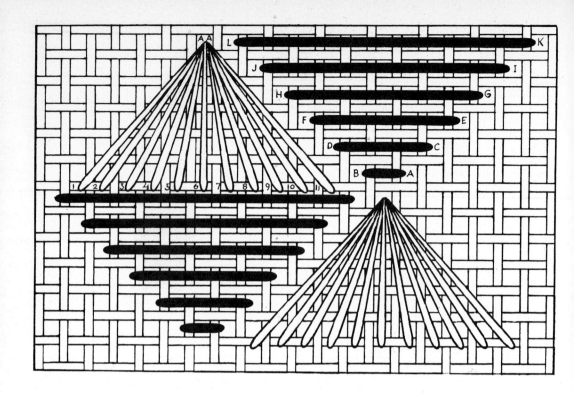

MONTENEGRIN
(Montenegrin cross, two-sided stitch)

The sample is worked on #12 Zweigart® Mono canvas with DMC® Floralia® (3-ply Persian yarn).

This braided stitch is worked in rows from left to right and is a combination of a long diagonal, a reversed half-cross, and an upright.

Begin with the long diagonal stitch worked over 2 horizontal and 4 vertical canvas threads (**1-2**). Then come back under 2 horizontal and 2 vertical canvas threads and work a reversed half-cross (**3-4**) *over* the long diagonal stitch. Come back under this stitch and work the upright stitch over 2 horizontal canvas threads *and* the long diagonal stitch. Repeat this sequence of stitches across the row. (See diagram.)

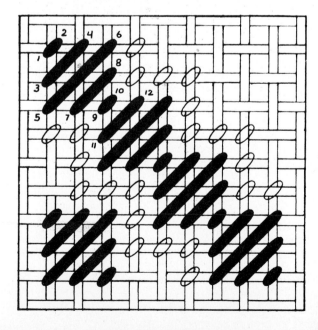

MOORISH

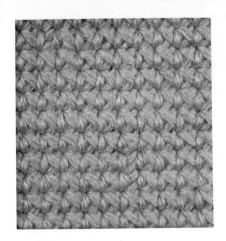

The sample is worked on #10 Zweigart® Mono canvas with DMC® Floralia® (3-ply Persian yarn).

The Moorish stitch consists of a variation of the Scotch stitch (page 130) worked in diagonal rows and separated by tent stitches on each side.

Begin at the upper left with a Scotch stitch worked over 3 horizontal and 3 vertical canvas threads (**1-2, 3-4, 5-6, 7-8**). Continue diagonally until the row is complete.

Next, in the same or a second color, work the tent stitches in groups of 3 as shown in the diagram.

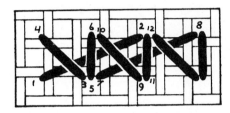

MOORISH, WIDE

The sample is worked on #14 Zweigart® Mono canvas with DMC® Floralia® (3-ply Persian yarn).

The Wide Moorish is a combination of the Moorish stitch and a separating row of Slanting 1 Gobelin (page 77).

It is stitched on the diagonal in 2 colors.

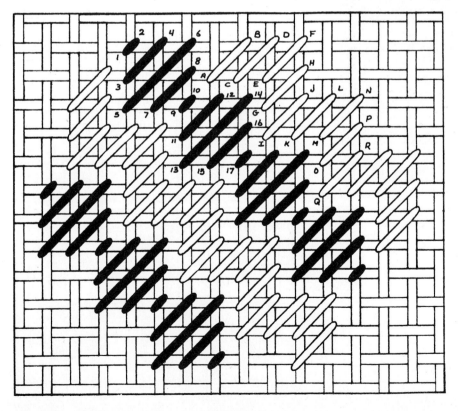

MOSAIC
(German)

The sample is worked on #10 Zweigart® Mono canvas with DMC® Floralia® (3-ply Persian yarn).

This is an excellent small-patterned background or border stitch. When it is worked in 2 colors, a checkerboard pattern is formed.

Each stitch unit is composed of 3 diagonal stitches. The first is worked over 1 horizontal and 1 vertical canvas thread, the second over 2 horizontal and 2 vertical canvas threads, and the third over 1 horizontal and 1 vertical canvas thread.

The Mosaic stitch can be worked in a horizontal or a vertical row (Diagram A) or diagonally (Diagram B).

This stitch will distort the canvas and should be worked on a frame.

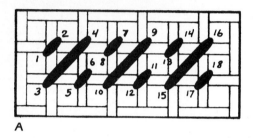

A

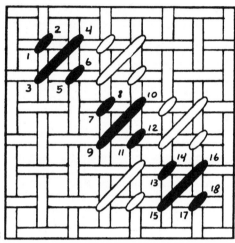

B

MOSAIC, CROSSED

The sample is worked on #14 Zweigart® Mono canvas with DMC® Floralia® (3-ply Persian yarn).

This is a combination of mosaic and diagonal stitches.

First, work the mosaic stitches in vertical rows (**1-2, 3-4, 5-6, 7-8,** etc.). Then work the crosses in a basketweave (diagonal) pattern (**A-B, C-D, E-F, G-H,** etc.).

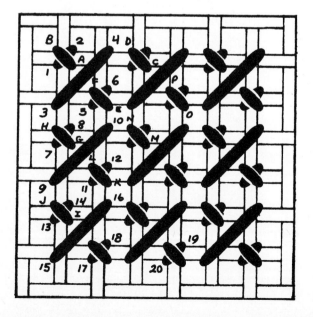

MOSAIC, DIAGONAL

The sample is worked on #12 Zweigart® Mono canvas with DMC® Floralia® (3-ply Persian yarn).

The Mosaic stitch worked diagonally is a favorite background stitch, although it does distort the canvas if not worked on a frame. This is one stitch that works well in alternating colored rows to create stripes.

The stitch unit is composed of 3 diagonal stitches worked over 2 horizontal and 2 vertical canvas threads (**1-2, 3-4, 5-6**). Notice that the third stitch is shared with and becomes the first stitch of the second unit. (See diagram.)

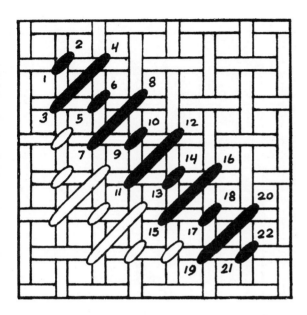

MOSAIC, REVERSED

The sample is worked on #10 Zweigart® Mono canvas with Anchor® Tapisserie (tapestry yarn).

This is a variation of the Mosaic stitch in which alternating units of the 3 diagonal stitches are worked diagonally from top left to bottom right (**1-2, 3-4, 5-6**) and the other alternating units are worked from top right to bottom left (**A-B, C-D, E-F**).

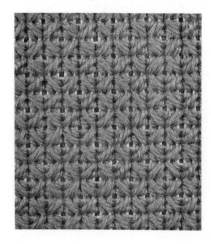

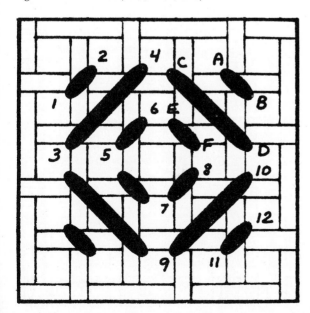

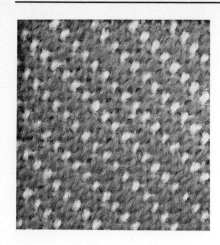

MOSAIC STRIPE

The sample is worked on #12 Zweigart® Mono canvas with DMC® Floralia® (3-ply Persian yarn).

This stitch is simply a Diagonal Mosaic stitch with a separating stripe of tent stitches.

Start by working the Mosaic stitch (**1-2, 3-4, 5-6, 7-8**, etc.). Next, work the tent stitches in a different color.

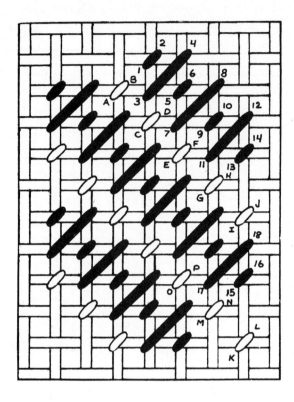

MOSAIC TILE

The sample is worked on #14 Zweigart® Mono canvas with Anchor® Tapisserie (tapestry yarn).

This stitch is a combination of a Mosaic stitch worked over 2 horizontal and 2 vertical canvas threads and a frame of 4 straight stitches enclosing the Mosaic stitch. It is worked in horizontal rows from right to left following the numbers on the diagram.

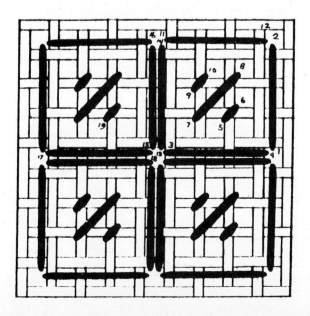

O

OBLONG CROSS

The sample is worked on #10 Zweigart® Mono canvas with DMC® Floralia® (3-ply Persian yarn).

The Oblong Cross-Stitch is an elongated variation of the cross-stitch that does not create a heavy backing. It can be worked on Mono or Penelope canvas.

First, work all the bottom stitches from left to right over 2 horizontal and 1 vertical canvas thread across the row (**1-2, 3-4, 5-6,** etc.). Then return, working the top stitches from right to left.

It is important to remember to work all the top stitches of the crosses in the same direction.

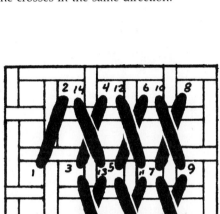

OBLONG CROSS WITH BACKSTITCH

The sample is worked on #10 Zweigart® Mono canvas with DMC® Floralia® (3-ply Persian yarn).

The Oblong Cross with Backstitch is similar to the previous stitch, with the addition of a small backstitch.

Work each stitch as a unit. First make an oblong cross over 1 vertical and 2 horizontal canvas threads (**1-2, 3-4**). Then work a small backstitch over 1 vertical canvas thread at the center of the cross (**5-6**).

This stitch produces a firm backing and uses a lot of yarn.

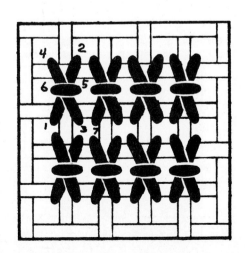

OBLONG RICE
(elongated crossed corners; rice, elongated; rice, oblong)

The sample is worked on #14 Zweigart® Mono canvas with DMC® Floralia® (3-ply Persian yarn).

This elongated version of the Rice stitch (page 123) is made by working an oblong cross over 4 horizontal and 2 vertical canvas threads, then crossing the corners of the stitch with small slanting or tie-down stitches over 2 horizontal and 1 vertical canvas threads. It can be worked in rows across the canvas with the tie stitches in a second color.

OCTAGON EYE
(octagonal eye, octagon eyelet)

The sample is worked on #14 Zweigart® Mono canvas with Anchor® Tapisserie (tapestry yarn).

This is an eyelet stitch framed with a backstitched perimeter shaped like an octagon.

Each leg of the eyelet is worked over 3 canvas threads ending in the center hole (**A**). Then a frame is backstitched across the 2 canvas threads at the outer points of the individual legs, forming the octagonal shape.

An extra backstitch is worked on the exposed canvas threads between 2 octagon eye stitches as shown in the diagram.

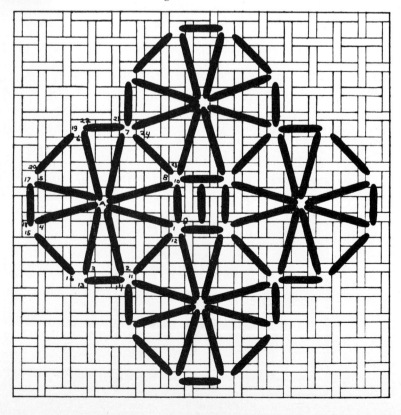

ORIENTAL

The sample is worked on #14 Zweigart® Mono canvas with DMC® Floralia® (3-ply Persian yarn).

The Oriental stitch resembles the Milanese stitch (page 100) and is often mistaken for it. This stitch is worked on the diagonal from upper left to lower right.

First, work the 4 diagonal stitches over 4, 3, 2, and 1 intersections of the vertical and horizontal canvas threads (**1-2, 3-4, 5-6, 7-8**). These will form the first triangle or arrowhead. Repeat this stitch until the diagonal row is completed. Next, work the return row of arrowheads in the same or a contrasting color with the arrowheads pointing in the opposite direction (up). Fill in the spaces between the rows with small diagonal stitches worked over 2 horizontal and 2 vertical canvas threads in the same color as the first row of arrowheads (**A-B, C-D,** etc.).

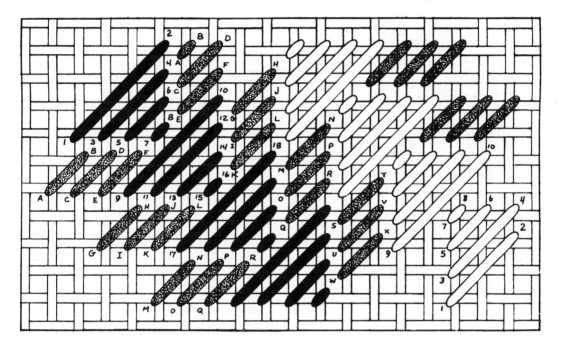

OUTLINE, WOVEN
(outline)

The sample is worked on #14 Zweigart® Mono canvas with DMC® Floralia® (3-ply Persian yarn).

There are a number of stitches that can be used to smooth out and cover the squared shapes and bared canvas threads left in needlepoint or canvas work. This stitch is the only one that can create a smooth curve.

First, work a uniform-size running stitch around the perimeter of the area or shape you want to outline. Next, loop a length of yarn under and over each of the running stitches as shown in the diagram.

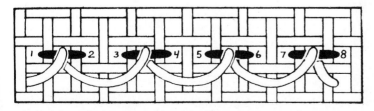

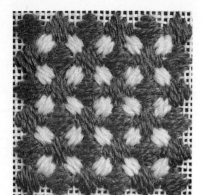

P

PALACE PATTERN

The sample is worked on #14 Zweigart® Mono canvas with DMC® Floralia® (3-ply Persian yarn).

This is a combination of ascending and descending straight stitches worked in horizontal and vertical blocks across horizontal rows (**1-2, 3-4, 5-6, 7-8, 9-10, 11-12,** etc.).

The diagonal stitches are worked *after* the rows of straight stitches are finished. They may be made in the same or a different yarn.

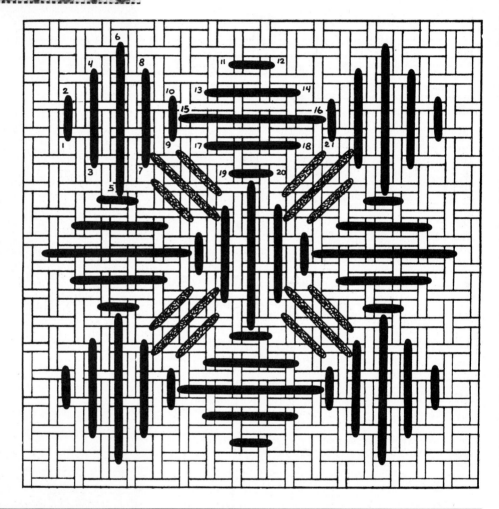

PARIS

The sample is worked on #10 Zweigart® Mono canvas with Anchor® Tapisserie (tapestry yarn).

This stitch resembles a woven basket.

Put 2 vertical straight stitches side by side in the same hole (**1-2, 3-4**). Then work a horizontal straight stitch over these 2 stitches and 2 vertical canvas threads (**5-6**). Continue across the row.

The second row is stepped 2 horizontal canvas threads down (**19-20**).

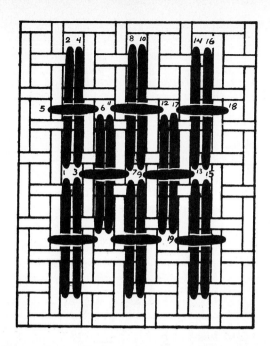

PARISIAN

The sample is worked on #10 Zweigart® Mono canvas with DMC® Floralia® (3-ply Persian yarn).

The Parisian stitch forms a pattern of alternating long and short stitches worked in a row over 2 and 4 horizontal canvas threads. The return row interlocks with the previous row, with the short stitch fitting under the long stitch and the long stitch fitting under the short stitch (see diagram). This stitch can be worked in 1 or 2 colors.

Do not confuse this stitch with the Hungarian stitch (page 84). There are no unworked canvas threads showing in this stitch.

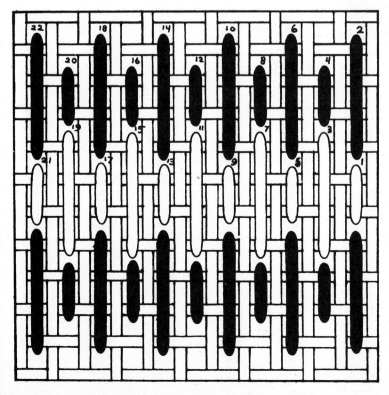

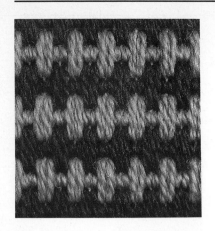

PARISIAN, DOUBLE

The sample is worked on #14 Zweigart® Mono canvas with DMC® Floralia® (3-ply Persian yarn).

The Double Parisian is a combination of long and short stitches over 2 and 4 or 4 and 6 horizontal canvas threads. Each stitch is worked twice, making the Parisian into a doubled stitch (**1-2, 3-4**).

Note that in Row 2, the long stitches are worked under the short stitches and the short stitches are under the long stitches.

This stitch can be worked in 1 color or in 2 colors to form a stripe pattern.

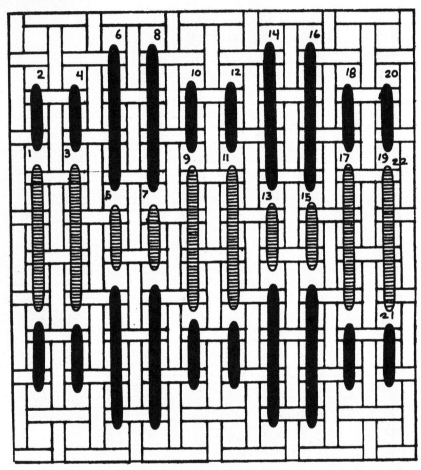

PAVILION, TIED
(tied, pavilion)

The sample is worked on #14 Zweigart® Mono canvas with DMC® Floralia® (3-ply Persian yarn).

The Pavilion stitch is an enlarged version of the Hungarian stitch (page 84). This stitch adds a short horizontal tied stitch placed in the center of each diamond over 2 vertical canvas threads.

First, work the diamonds over 2, 4, 6, 8, 6, 4, and 2 horizontal canvas threads (**1-2, 3-4, 5-6, 7-8,** etc.) across the row. Then, return and place the tied stitches in the center of each diamond (**A-B, C-D,** etc.).

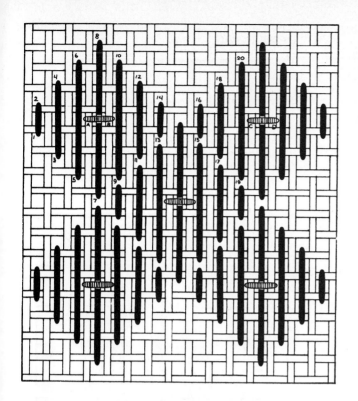

PAVILION, TIED (WITH BACKSTITCH)
(tied pavilion with backstitch)

The sample is worked on #14 Zweigart® Mono canvas with DMC® Floralia® (3-ply Persian yarn).

This stitch is worked exactly as the Tied Pavilion with the addition of a backstitch placed around the outer edge of the diamonds, as shown in white on the diagram.

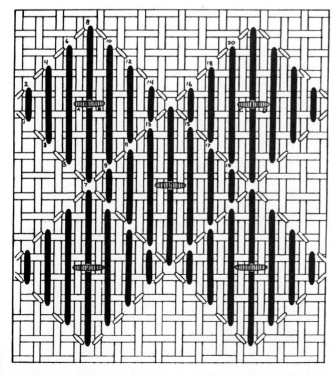

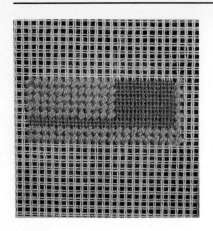

PETIT POINT

The sample is worked on #14 Zweigart® Penelope canvas with Anchor® floss.

To work Petit Point on Penelope canvas it is necessary to split the vertical canvas threads and then work in the Continental (page 144) stitch (as in diagram) or the Basketweave (page 144) stitch.

This canvas is used only when the majority of the work is done in the larger stitch and a small area is to be worked in Petit Point.

To work an entire piece in Petit Point, use silk gauze instead of Penelope canvas.

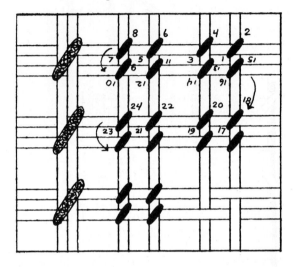

PINEAPPLE

The sample is worked on #12 Zweigart® Mono canvas with DMC® Floralia® (3-ply Persian yarn).

This stitch is a Gobelin variation with 4 Upright Gobelin stitches (page 79) worked over 4 horizontal canvas threads. Then, a Cross-Stitch (page 45) is placed *over* the Gobelin stitches. Finally, a small tent stitch is worked over the center vertical canvas thread.

The stitch is worked in horizontal rows from right to left (see diagram).

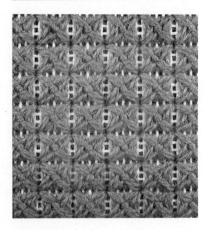

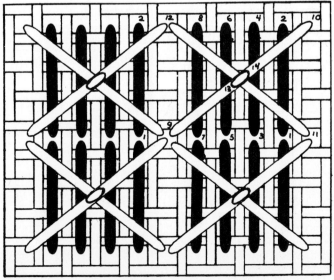

PINEAPPLE, ALTERNATING
(chessboard)

The sample is worked on #12 Zweigart® Mono canvas with Anchor® Tapisserie (tapestry yarn).

This stitch is similar to the Pineapple stitch.

Work 4 upright straight stitches over 4 horizontal canvas threads. Then, add a cross-stitch over the 4 upright stitches covering 4 horizontal and 3 vertical canvas threads. Add a horizontal stitch over the center of the cross covering 1 vertical thread.

Now work a unit of 4 upright stitches next to the first set of stitches. Do not add a cross-stitch.

Repeat these 2 units across the row.

To work the second row, place the cross-stitch unit below the plain upright-stitch unit. This produces the chessboard pattern.

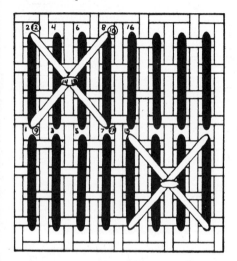

PINEAPPLE, STEPPED
(pineapple, half-drop)

The sample is worked on #12 Zweigart® Mono canvas with DMC® Floralia® (3-ply Persian yarn).

This variation of the Pineapple stitch is worked diagonally and produces a totally different appearance. Starting at the lower right corner, each unit is placed 2 canvas threads above the preceding unit. (See diagram.)

Each unit is worked exactly as the Pineapple stitch.

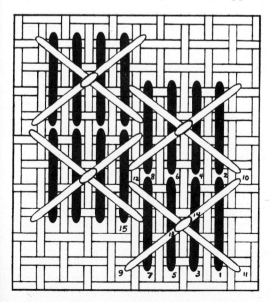

PORTUGUESE
(Portuguese border, Portuguese filling)

The sample is worked on #14 Zweigart® Mono canvas with DMC® Floralia® (3-ply Persian yarn) and Anchor® floss.

This stitch is a combination of a vertical row of horizontal stitches and stem stitches.

Begin by working a vertical row of horizontal stitches over 7 vertical canvas threads, leaving 3 horizontal canvas threads between the stitches (**1-2, 3-4, 5-6, 7-8, 9-10**, etc.).

Then, beginning at the bottom, work a series of stem stitches over these horizontal stitches without piercing the canvas.

Start with 4 satin stitches over the bottom 2 horizontal stitches (**11-12, 13-14**, etc.). Then 2 stem stitches are worked over and under the second and third horizontal stitches, continuing upward as shown in the diagram (**19-20, 21-22**). Continue to the top of the row, then start again at the bottom and repeat for the right side.

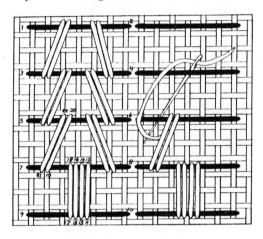

PORTUGUESE STEM
(Portuguese knotted stem)

The sample is worked on #14 Zweigart® Mono canvas with DMC® Floralia® (3-ply Persian yarn).

This stitch produces a knotted raised line or group of vertical stripes when worked in rows.

Begin at the lower edge, working an oblique stitch over 1 vertical and 4 horizontal canvas threads (Diagram A, **1-2**). Then, slip the needle under this stitch from right to left (Diagram B), wrapping the yarn around the stitch firmly. Next, repeat this wrapping stitch just below the first wrapping stitch (Diagram C).

Place a second oblique stitch 2 horizontal canvas threads above the top of the first oblique stitch (Diagram D). Repeat the wrapping as shown in Diagram E, working over the top of the first and the bottom of the second oblique stitch.

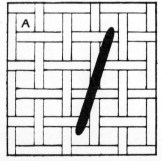

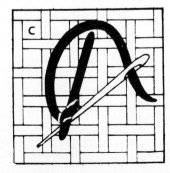

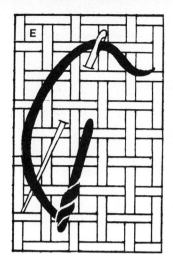

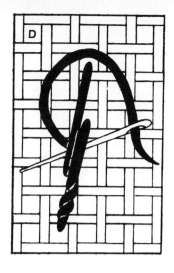

R

REP

The sample is worked on #14 Zweigart® Penelope canvas with Anchor® floss.

The Rep stitch forms a small vertical stripe. It can be worked in 1 color horizontally (see diagram) or in 2 colors vertically to form a pinstripe.

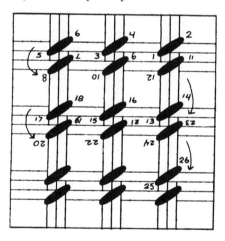

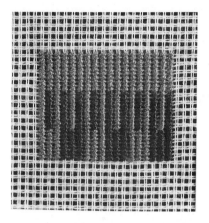

REVERSED TENT
(knitting tent, tent reversed)

The sample is worked on #12 Zweigart® Mono canvas with DMC® Floralia® (3-ply Persian yarn).

The Reversed Tent stitch is a combination of the Half-Cross stitch (page 145) and a reversed half-cross stitch worked in 2 vertical or horizontal rows of stitches slanting in opposite directions. (See diagram.)

It can be worked in 1 color as a background or 2 colors to form stripes or even a basket pattern.

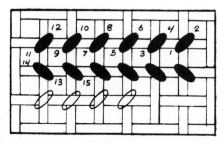

RHODES

The sample is worked on #14 Zweigart® Mono canvas with Anchor® floss.

The Rhodes stitch was created by British designer, teacher, and author Mary Rhodes.

This is a heavy square stitch that can be worked over an area from 3 to 24 or more horizontal and vertical canvas threads.

The sample is worked over 6 horizontal and vertical canvas threads.

To work, make a stitch starting 1 canvas thread from the lower left-hand corner at **1**, passing over the center hole of the square, coming down 1 vertical thread to the left of the top right-hand corner at **2**. Continue in this manner around the square, always working in the same direction until every hole is used. End with a diagonal stitch from the top right-hand corner to the bottom left-hand corner (**23-24**).

RHODES, CROSSED CORNER

The sample is worked on #14 Zweigart® Mono canvas with Anchor® floss.

This is a variation of the Rhodes stitch with 4 diagonal stitches worked over the original Rhodes stitch at each corner. Place the diagonal stitch from the center hole at the top to the center hole at each side and the center hole at the bottom to the same center hole at each side.

The diagonal stitches are often used to stabilize a very large Rhodes stitch.

RHODES, DIAMOND

The sample is worked on Zweigart® Congress cloth with Anchor® floss.

The Diamond Rhodes can be worked over any *even* number of canvas threads.

Start at the bottom point of the diamond, going up to the top point of the diamond (**1-2**). Working around to the right on the diagonal, make 4 more stitches (**3-4, 5-6, 7-8, 9-10**). Then, place a horizontal stitch across from the right to the left points of the diamond (**11-12**). Continue around and make 4 more stitches on the diagonal (**13-14, 15-16, 17-18, 19-20**).

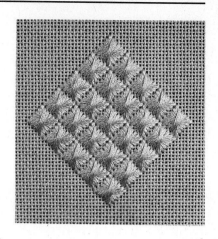

RHODES, HALF

The sample is worked on #14 Zweigart® Mono canvas with Anchor® floss.

This stitch is *half* a Rhodes stitch and is worked in horizontal rows. It can be made over any *even* number of canvas threads.

The spaces between the stitches can be filled with tent or horizontal straight stitches.

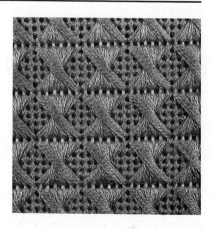

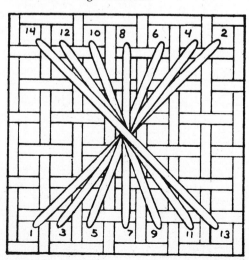

119

RHODES, HALF HALF-DROP

The sample is worked on #14 Zweigart® Mono canvas with Anchor® floss.

The Half Half-Drop Rhodes is a Half-Stitch Rhodes worked in diagonal rows over any even number of canvas threads.

The sample is worked over 4 horizontal and vertical canvas threads.

Work the first Half-Stitch Rhodes as shown in the diagram. The second half-stitch starts 2 horizontal threads down and 1 vertical thread to the left of the bottom of the last stitch at **11**.

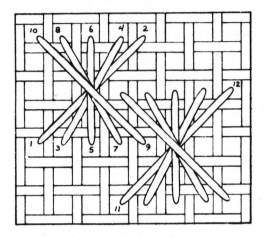

RHODES, HEART

The sample is worked on #14 Zweigart® Mono canvas with Anchor® floss.

This Rhodes stitch variation forms the shape of a heart. It is a bulky stitch worked across the shape of the heart from edge to edge.

It is essential to follow the numbering in the diagram *exactly*. Any variation will change the outcome.

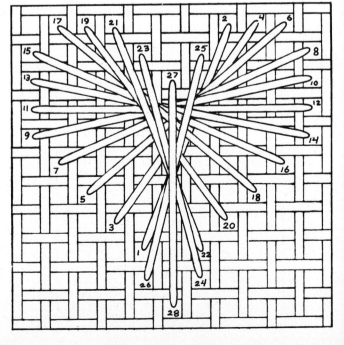

RHODES, OCTAGONAL

The sample is worked on Zweigart® Congress cloth with Anchor® floss.

This variation of the Rhodes stitch is worked in an octagonal shape. It can be worked only over a multiple of 4 canvas threads. The sample was made over 16 horizontal and vertical canvas threads.

First, work the 7 stitches from top to bottom (**1-2, 3-4, 5-6, 7-8,** etc.) as in the Half-Stitch Rhodes. Next, 4 stitches are worked diagonally from the bottom right to the top left (**15-16, 17-18, 19-20, 21-22**). Continue around, working 7 stitches from the right to the left side (**23-24 to 35-36**).

To finish, work 4 more diagonal stitches from the top right to the bottom left (**37-38, 39-40, 41-42, 43-44**).

The spaces between the stitches can be filled with a Diamond Rhodes.

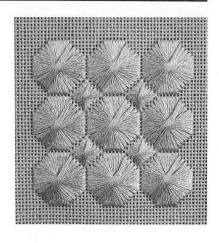

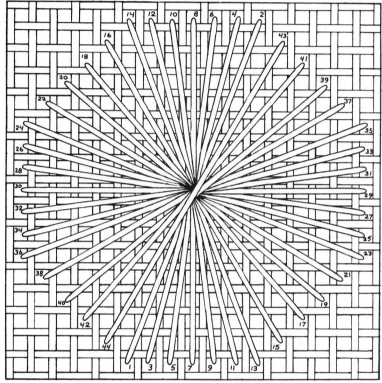

RHODES, TIED

The sample is worked on #14 Zweigart® Mono canvas with DMC® #3 perle cotton.

The Tied Rhodes stitch is worked exactly as the Rhodes stitch with a small vertical stitch added at the center to tie the stitch. This tie stitch is worked over 2 horizontal canvas threads.

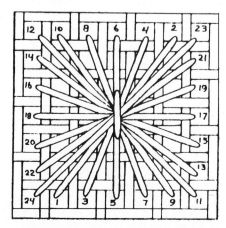

RIBBED SQUARE
(ringed square)

The sample is worked on #10 Zweigart® Mono canvas with DMC® Floralia® (3-ply Persian yarn).

The Ribbed Square can be used as a decorative motif or an allover texture pattern.

Begin by working a Cross-Stitch over 12 horizontal and 12 vertical canvas threads and an Upright Cross (page 50) over the same 12 horizontal and 12 vertical canvas threads (see diagram). Next, work the 8 small stitches over 2 and 3 canvas threads as shown in the diagram. Bring the needle forward to the front as close to the center as possible between any 2 legs of any of the crosses. Working in a counterclockwise direction, weave the yarn over the first leg and under it and the next leg. Continue around in this manner until you meet the small stitches. Then continue around, including these stitches in the weaving until the outer edge is reached and the stitch is completed.

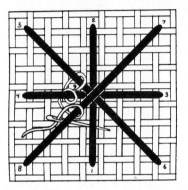

RIBBED SQUARE SPIDER

The sample is worked on #10 Zweigart® Mono canvas with DMC® Floralia® (3-ply Persian yarn).

All Ribbed Spider stitches are attractive when used as an individual motif, but they can be grouped to form an allover pattern. This variation produces a squared motif.

First, work the Upright Cross (page 50) over 8 canvas threads (**1-2, 3-4**), then a cross-stitch on top (**5-6, 7-8**), forming a squared underlayment. (See diagram.)

Next, bring the needle up from the back between any 2 legs of any of the crosses, close to the center. Now weave under and over the legs on *top* of the canvas in a counterclockwise direction, working under 2 and over 1 leg until they are all covered. Keep pushing the woven rounds toward the center as you work.

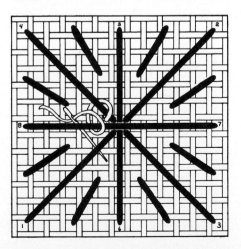

RICE
(William and Mary, crossed corners)

The sample is worked on #12 Zweigart® Mono canvas with DMC® Floralia® (3-ply Persian yarn).

The Rice stitch is a Cross-Stitch (page 45) with tied legs. It is very effective to work the cross in one color and the tied stitches in another color.

First, work the cross-stitch over 2 horizontal and 2 vertical canvas threads (1-2, 3-4). Next, work the tie stitches at the end of each leg over 1 horizontal and 1 vertical canvas thread.

This stitch can be worked in horizontal or vertical rows and makes an excellent background, filling, or border stitch.

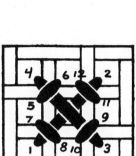

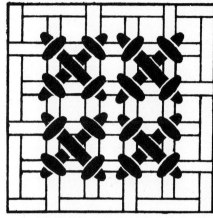

RICE, STRAIGHT

The sample is worked on #12 Zweigart® Mono canvas with Anchor® Tapisserie (tapestry yarn).

This is a variation of the Rice stitch.

First, work an Upright Cross (page 50) over 4 vertical (1-2) and 4 horizontal (3-4) canvas threads. Next, make a Backstitch (page 26) over 2 canvas threads at the end of each leg of the upright cross.

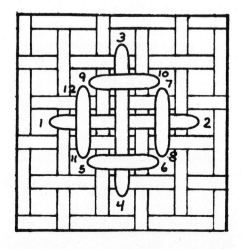

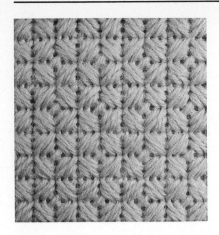

RICE, TRIPLE

The sample is worked on #12 Zweigart® Mono canvas with Anchor® Tapisserie (tapestry yarn).

This attractive variation of the Rice stitch can be used as an individual motif or an allover pattern.

The underlayment is a cross-stitch worked over 6 horizontal and 6 vertical canvas threads (**1-2, 3-4**). Then the 3 diagonal stitches are worked over *each* leg of the cross (**5-6, 7-8, 9-10**). See the diagram for the direction of these diagonal stitches.

RICKRACK

The sample is worked on #12 Zweigart® Mono canvas with DMC® Floralia® (3-ply Persian yarn).

This stitch is worked in horizontal rows across the canvas.

Begin by working a row of 2 horizontal straight stitches over 4 vertical canvas threads (**1-2, 3-4, 5-6, 7-8**, etc.). Next, work a vertical stitch over 3 horizontal canvas threads in the space between the groups of horizontal stitches (**9-10, 11-12, 13-14**, etc.). Finally, work a diagonal stitch over the first 3 horizontal stitches (**15-16, 17-18, 19-20**) across the row and cross it with a second diagonal stitch on the return journey.

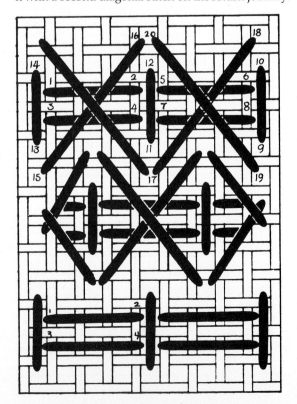

RIDGE
(oblique cross)

The sample is worked on #14 Zweigart® Mono canvas with DMC® Floralia® (3-ply Persian yarn).

This stitch forms a vertical stripe pattern.

Work in vertical rows starting at the upper left-hand corner. Begin with an oblique stitch over 2 horizontal and 4 vertical canvas threads (**1-2**). Next, cross the first stitch working over 4 horizontal and 2 vertical canvas threads (**3-4**). (See diagram.)

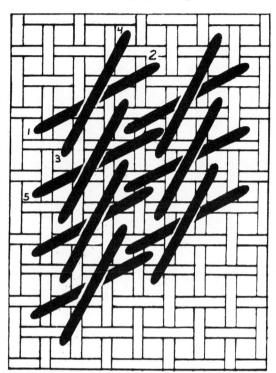

ROCOCO

The sample is worked on #12 Zweigart® Mono canvas with Anchor® Tapisserie (tapestry yarn).

The Rococo stitch is made of 4 upright stitches, worked over 4 horizontal canvas threads that share the same hole at the top and bottom. These 4 upright stitches are tied with small horizontal stitches placed over 1 vertical thread in the center.

This stitch works best on the diagonal (see diagram).

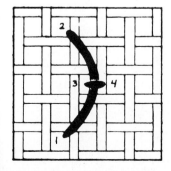

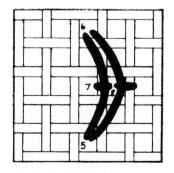

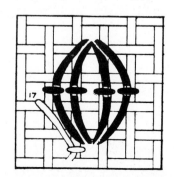

ROMAN II

The sample is worked on #10 Zweigart® Mono canvas with Anchor® Tapisserie (tapestry yarn).

This stitch is made of 2 straight stitches worked over 4 horizontal canvas threads stepped diagonally.

A horizontal straight stitch worked over 3 vertical canvas threads is placed above and below the straight stitches to form the Roman numeral II (two).

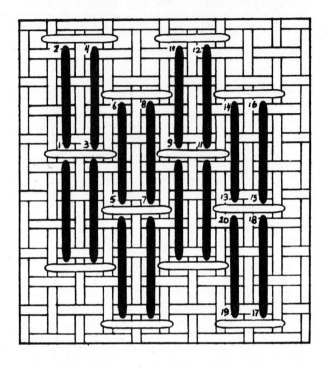

ROMAN III

The sample is worked on #14 Zweigart® Mono canvas with DMC® Floralia® (3-ply Persian yarn).

The Roman III looks like the Roman numeral three with groups of 3 vertical stitches placed over 3 horizontal canvas threads in a descending stepped pattern (**1-2, 3-4, 5-6, 7-8,** etc.).

When all the vertical stitches are completed, work the horizontal stitches in a second color over 4 vertical canvas threads (**A-B, C-D, E-F,** etc.).

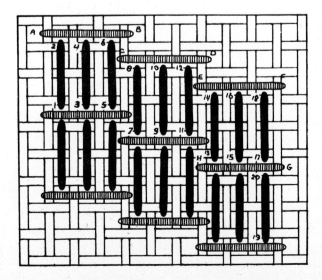

ROSEBUD
(minileaf)

The sample is worked on #14 Zweigart® Mono canvas with DMC® Floralia® (3-ply Persian yarn).

This stitch looks like a leaf when worked in 1 color and a rosebud when worked in floral tones (red, pink, yellow, etc.) with 2 tones of green to form the calyx of the bud.

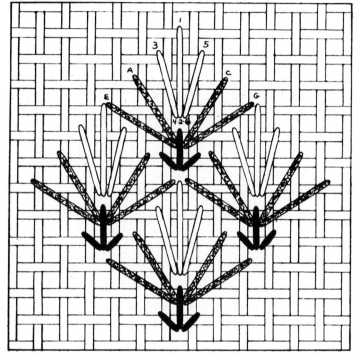

ROUMANIAN COUCHING

The sample is worked on #10 Zweigart® Mono canvas with Anchor® Tapisserie (tapestry yarn) and Anchor® floss.

First, lay a long horizontal stitch across any number of vertical canvas threads (1-2). This long horizontal stitch is then tied with diagonal stitches crossing 1 horizontal and 3 vertical canvas threads. The placement of these tie stitches will produce a pattern and can make diagonal (see diagram) or vertical stripes. Try working the tie stitches in a contrasting color.

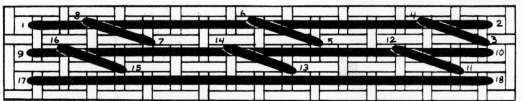

S

SATIN, PADDED

The sample is worked on #12 Zweigart® Mono canvas with DMC® Floralia® (3-ply Persian yarn).

This stitch is made of 10 horizontal straight stitches graduated in size to form a triangle pointing to the left and, next to it, another group of 10 horizontal straight stitches graduated to form a triangle pointing to the right (**1-2, 3-4,** etc.).

To pad the stitch, bring the yarn to the top of the first stitch at **A** and weave down under the right-hand group of stitches (**B**), around and under the left-hand group of stitches (**C**). This may be repeated 2 or 3 or more times until the desired amount of padding has been obtained. Return the needle to the back at point **A**.

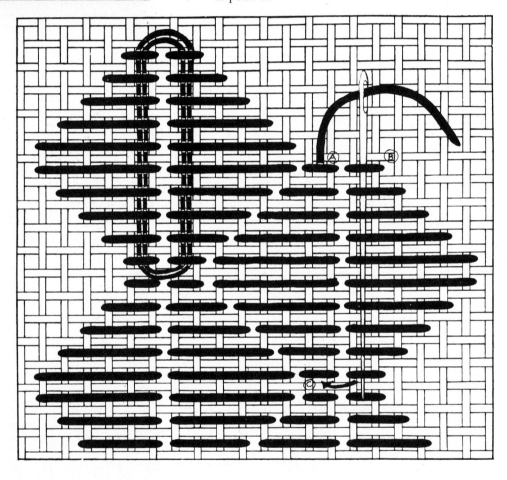

SATIN TRIANGLES

The sample is worked on #14 Zweigart® Mono canvas with DMC® Floralia® (3-ply Persian yarn).

This stitch alternates horizontal and vertical stitch triangle shapes.

First, work 6 horizontal straight stitches over 2, 4, 6, 8, 10, and 12 vertical canvas threads (**1-2, 3-4, 5-6,** etc.). Make a row of these triangles horizontally across the area to be covered.

Next, fill in the spaces between these triangles by working 11 vertical straight stitches over 1, 2, 3, 4, 5, 6, 5, 4, 3, 2, and 1 horizontal canvas threads (**A-B, C-D, E-F,** etc.).

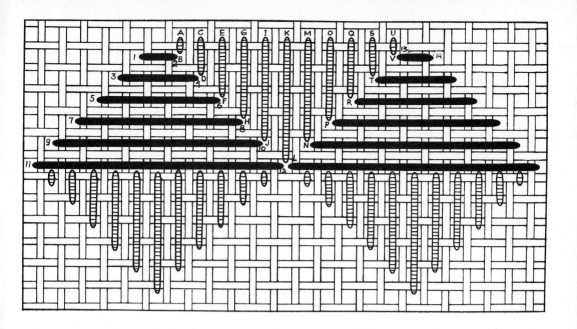

SATIN TRIANGLES VARIATION

The sample is worked on #12 Zweigart® Mono canvas with DMC® Floralia® (3-ply Persian yarn).

Start this pattern by working a cross-stitch over 2 horizontal and 2 vertical canvas threads (**1-2, 3-4**). Then, frame the cross with 8 backstitches, each over 1 canvas thread (**a, b, c, d, e, f, g, h**).

Next, work a group of 5 straight stitches (**5-6, 7-8, 9-10, 11-12, 13-14**) over 2, 3, 4, 3, and 2 canvas threads, forming a triangle. Work the next cross with backstitch (**15-16,** etc.), turn the canvas counterclockwise, and repeat the instructions for the triangle.

Continue in this manner until all 4 triangles are worked. *Note:* The crosses with backstitch become the side of the next stitch. (See diagram.)

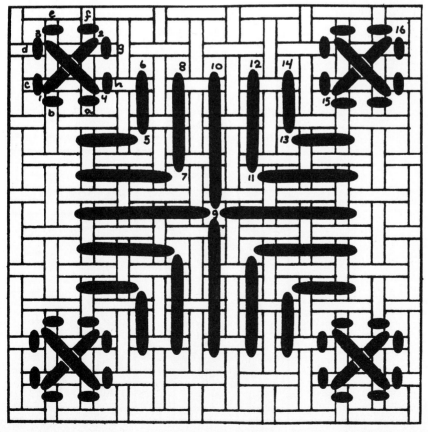

SCOTCH
(cushion, diagonal satin, flat, Scottish)

The sample is worked on #12 Zweigart® Mono canvas with DMC® Floralia® (3-ply Persian yarn).

This is one of the most popular and versatile stitches known to canvas needleworkers. It is called by many names, as shown above, and there are many variations used in combination with other stitches. This square stitch can be worked horizontally or vertically.

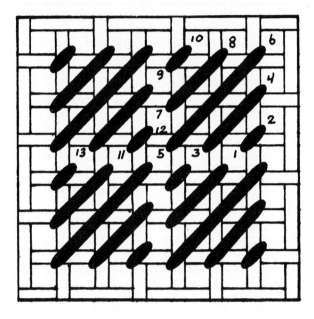

SCOTCH, ALTERNATING
(alternating cushion, cushion variation, reversed cushion, reversed flat)

The sample is worked on #10 Zweigart® Mono canvas with Anchor® Tapisserie (tapestry yarn).

The Alternating Scotch stitch is really four 5-stitch Scotch stitches placed in alternating directions to form a square. It is worked diagonally as shown in the diagram.

This stitch can be worked in 1 or 2 colors. It will distort the canvas and should be worked on a frame.

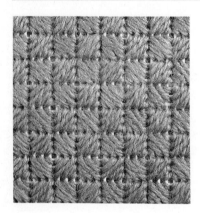

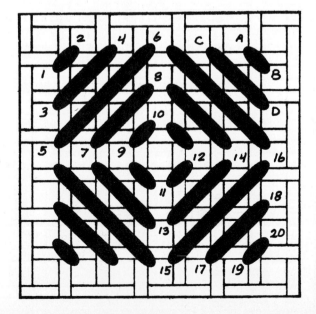

SCOTCH, BORDERED ALTERNATING

The sample is worked on #12 Zweigart® Mono Canvas with DMC® Floralia® (3-ply Persian yarn).

The Bordered Alternating Scotch stitch is a variation of the Alternating Scotch stitch with a border of Straight Gobelin stitches worked over 2 canvas threads.

Start by working the horizontal rows of alternating Scotch stitches over 3 horizontal and 3 vertical canvas threads (**A-B, C-D, E-F,** etc.), leaving 2 vertical canvas threads between the alternating Scotch squares.

Next, fill in the border straight Gobelin stitches using the same color, a different color, or a different thread (floss) of the same color (**1-2, 3-4, 5-6,** etc.).

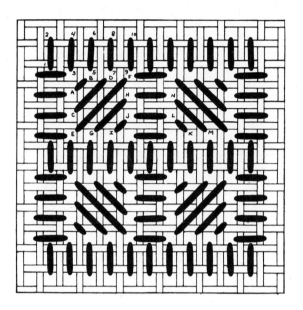

SCOTCH, CROSS-CORNERED
(cross-cornered cushion)

The sample is worked on #12 Mono canvas with Anchor® Tapisserie (tapestry yarn).

The Cross-Cornered Scotch stitch can be worked as a border or frame or as a single motif in a large version of the stitch.

It is made of 4 Scotch stitches turned to have the long stitch of each unit share a center hole. The individual units are worked over 3 horizontal and 3 vertical canvas threads. Then a half-Scotch is worked on the diagonal, *over* the 4 Scotch stitches as shown in the diagram.

The top-laid stitches may be worked in the same or a different color.

131

SCOTCH, FRAMED
(framed cushion)

The sample is worked on #10 Zweigart® Mono canvas with Anchor® Tapisserie (tapestry yarn).

This variation is a Scotch stitch completely surrounded by tent stitches.

All the diagonal stitches in this combination stitch must slant in the same direction. The tent stitches can be worked in the same or a contrasting color.

This stitch will distort the canvas and should be worked on a frame.

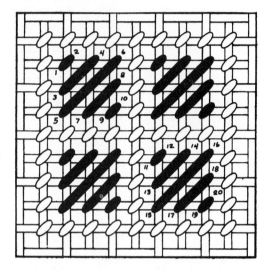

SCOTCH, FRAMED CHECKER

The sample is worked on #14 Zweigart® Mono canvas with DMC® Floralia® (3-ply Persian yarn) and DMC #5 perle cotton.

The Framed Checker stitch consists of the Scotch stitch alternated with diagonal rows of squares of 4 tent stitches and framed with backstitches placed between the rows.

First, work the row of Scotch stitches (**1-2, 3-4, 5-6,** etc.). Then, add the squares of tent stitches in the same yarn, in the same color or a different color, or in another thread, such as silk or cotton floss.

The Backstitch is added over 2 canvas threads *after* the entire area is stitched. It looks better when worked in a different thread or a lighter-weight yarn.

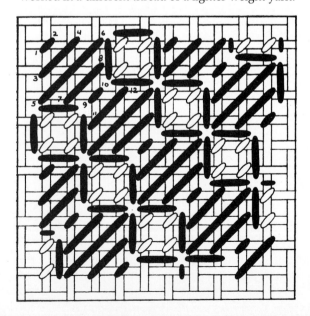

SCOTCH I, ALTERNATING

The sample is worked on #10 Zweigart® Mono canvas with Anchor® Tapisserie (tapestry yarn) and Anchor® floss.

The Alternating Scotch I is worked in vertical rows, with the stitches in each row of squares slanting in two different diagonal directions.

This stitch can be worked in 1 color, 2 colors, or 2 types of embroidery thread, such as wool or cotton floss.

Start with the first yarn or thread and complete the row of half-squares (**1-2, 3-4, 5-6, 7-8, 9-10,** etc.). Change to the second color or thread and complete each square (**A-B, C-D, E-F,** etc.).

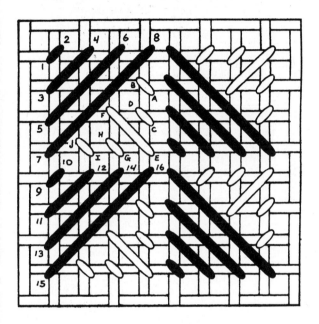

SCOTCH II, ALTERNATING

The sample is worked on #10 Zweigart® Mono canvas with DMC® Floralia® (3-ply Persian yarn) and Anchor ® floss.

The Alternating Scotch II stitch is worked exactly as the Alternating Scotch I stitch, with the slant of the diagonal stitches worked in facing directions in sets of 2 vertical rows.

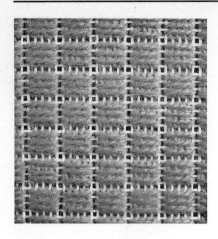

SEVEN
(fences)

The sample is worked on #12 Zweigart® Mono canvas with DMC® Floralia® (3-ply Persian yarn).

This stitch forms a vertical stripe pattern.

First, work 4 upright stitches over 4 horizontal canvas threads (**1-2, 3-4, 5-6, 7-8**). Next, work 3 horizontal stitches over 5 vertical canvas threads and the 4 upright stitches (see diagram).

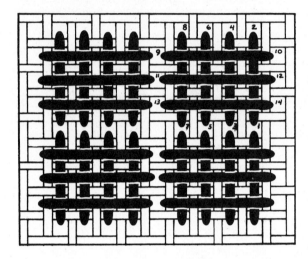

SHELL
(sheaf)

The sample is worked on #12 Zweigart® Mono canvas with DMC® Floralia® (3-ply Persian yarn).

The Shell stitch consists of 4 upright stitches worked over 4–6 horizontal canvas threads (**1-2, 3-4, 5-6, 7-8**) and pulled together in the middle with a backstitch that is placed to the left of the center vertical canvas thread (**9**), wrapped around the 4 upright stitches, and brought to the back at **10**.

An Upright Cross or Gobelin stitch can be placed in the spaces between the shells to cover the exposed canvas threads.

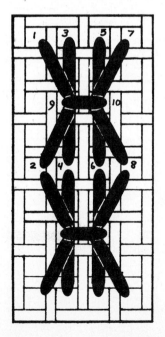

SHELL, LOOPED

The sample is worked on #12 Zweigart® Mono canvas with Anchor® Tapisserie (tapestry yarn).

The Looped Shell stitch is made of Wheatsheaf stitches (page 154) worked in a horizontal row joined by a woven loop.

Start by working 4 vertical straight stitches over 6 horizontal canvas threads (**1-2, 3-4, 5-6, 7-8**). Come up from the back at **9** (Diagram A), over 1 vertical canvas thread and the 4 straight stitches just made, and down at **10**. Repeat for **11-12** (Diagram B). Continue across the row.

Change color and come up at **A**, weave through (**9-10, 11-12**), on both Wheatsheaf stitches (Diagram C). Repeat 1 more time (Diagram D).

A

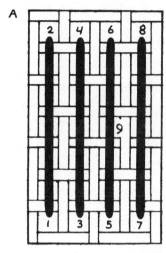

B

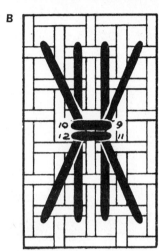

C

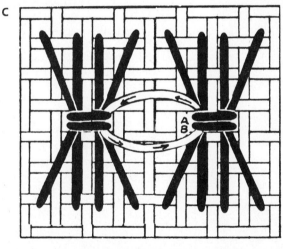

D

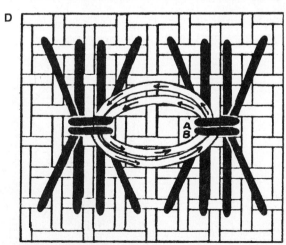

SMYRNA, ALTERNATING

The sample is worked on #10 Zweigart® Mono canvas with Anchor® Tapisserie (tapestry yarn).

The Alternating Smyrna is worked over 2 horizontal and 2 vertical canvas threads in double rows covering 3 horizontal canvas threads.

Work the first Smyrna stitch (**1-2, 3-4, 5-6, 7-8**). Then, starting 1 horizontal thread down and 2 vertical canvas threads to the left, work the second stitch (**9-10, 11-12, 13-14, 15-16**). Repeat these 2 stitches across the row. (See diagram.)

Work this stitch in 1 color.

SMYRNA, LINKED
(long-arm Smyrna, tied Smyrna)

The sample is worked on #12 Zweigart® Mono canvas with DMC® Floralia® (3-ply Persian yarn).

This is a variation of the Smyrna stitch in which 2 Smyrna units are joined or linked by 1 long horizontal stitch.

First, work the vertical stitch of the upright cross over 4 horizontal canvas threads (**1-2**). Then, place a cross-stitch over 4 horizontal and 4 vertical canvas threads on top of the vertical stitch (**3-4, 5-6**). Now, work a second Smyrna unit next to the first and tie them together with a long horizontal stitch (**13-14**). (See Diagram A.)

The Linked Smyrna is worked in horizontal rows. The second row is offset one-half stitch (see Diagram B).

A

B

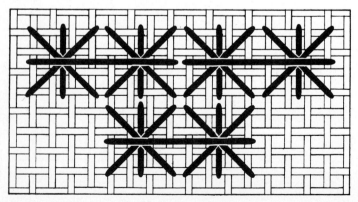

SMYRNA CROSS
(double cross, leviathan)

The sample is worked on #14 Zweigart® Mono canvas with DMC® Floralia® (3-ply Persian yarn).

The Smyrna Cross-Stitch can be worked over 2, 4, 6, or 8 horizontal and vertical canvas threads; however, the larger stitch will leave exposed canvas threads.

First, work a Cross-Stitch over 2 horizontal and 2 vertical canvas threads (**1-2, 3-4**). Then work an upright cross on top of the first cross (**5-6, 7-8**).

Always cross the top stitches in the same direction. This stitch can be worked in 2 colors, using 1 color for the cross stitch and another for the upright cross.

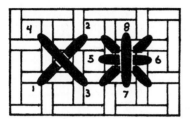

SPRAT
(tailor tack)

The sample is worked on #14 Zweigart® Mono canvas with DMC® Floralia® (3-ply Persian yarn).

This needlework adaptation of the familiar tailor's tacking stitch can be used as a border or a background stitch. It gives a woven appearance.

Work the first stitch over 3 horizontal and vertical canvas threads (**1-2**). The second stitch is started 6 vertical canvas threads to the right of the first stitch (**3-4**). The third, fourth, fifth, and sixth stitches must be carefully placed to cross *over* the first and second stitches. (See Diagram A, stitches **5-6, 7-8, 9-10, 11-12**.)

Diagram B shows the placement of the surrounding stitches when used as an allover pattern.

A

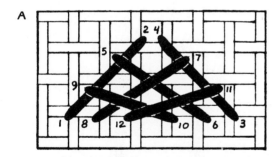

B

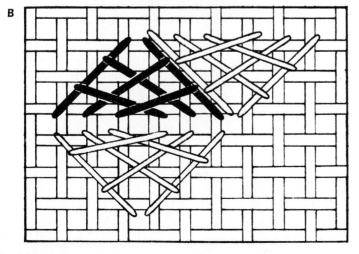

SPRINGS
(spring)

The sample is worked on #12 Zweigart® Mono canvas with Anchor® Tapisserie (tapestry yarn).

The Springs stitch is used as an allover filling, border or background pattern.

First, work an elongated cross-stitch over 10 horizontal and 3 vertical canvas threads. Then, put a vertical unit of 5 horizontal stitches over 3 vertical canvas threads starting 3 horizontal canvas threads down from the top of the cross. To complete, a small cross-stitch is worked in the "V" formed at the top and bottom of the elongated cross over 2 horizontal and 1 vertical canvas threads.

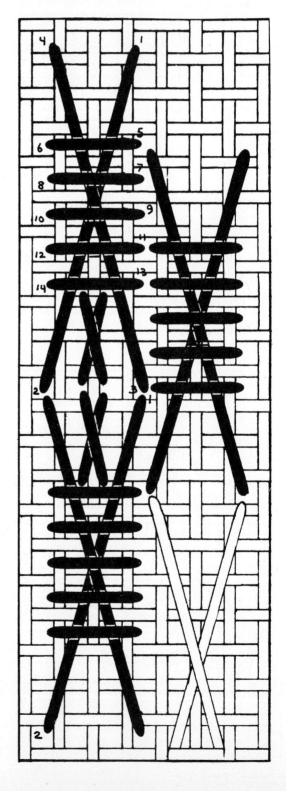

STAR, DOUBLE

The sample is worked on #12 Zweigart® Mono canvas with DMC® Floralia® (3-ply Persian yarn).

This stitch is a Reversed Mosaic (page 105) with a frame worked in a second color.

Following the numbers in the diagram carefully, first work the reversed mosaic stitches across the row (**1-2, 3-4, 5-6**, etc.).

Then add the straight stitches or frame.

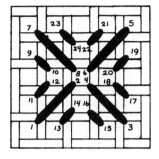 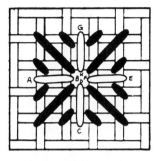

STAR, FRAMED

The sample is worked on #10 Zweigart® Mono canvas with DMC® Floralia® (3-ply Persian yarn).

This is a variation of the star stitch with a frame added to cover the exposed canvas threads.

The stars may be worked in 1 color with a contrasting frame, or as an allover pattern with each star a different color.

Experiment—this is a fun pattern.

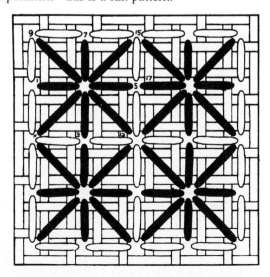

STAR, SLANTING
(star of Bethlehem)

The sample is worked on #12 Zweigart® Mono canvas with DMC® Floralia® (3-ply Persian yarn).

The Slanting Star is worked on a background of cross-stitches. First, work the cross-stitches over the intersection of 1 vertical and 1 horizontal canvas thread. Complete the entire background.

Then, place a diagonal stitch over 4 horizontal and 4 vertical canvas threads (**1-2**). Next, work an upright cross over the center of the diagonal stitch (**3-4, 5-6**).

Finish with a diagonal stitch over 2 horizontal and 2 vertical canvas threads over the center of the upright cross, slanting to the left. (See diagram.)

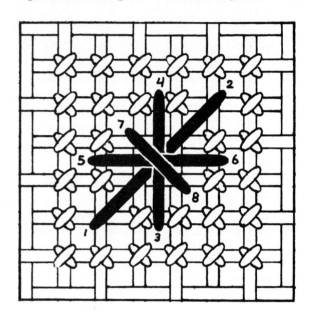

STEM
(long oblique)

The sample is worked on #14 Zweigart® Mono canvas with DMC® Floralia® (3-ply Persian yarn).

This is a combination of the Slanting 2 Gobelin stitch (page 77) and a Backstitch.

Two vertical rows of slanting Gobelin stitches are worked in opposite directions over 2 horizontal and 2 vertical canvas threads. The backstitch is put in (see diagram for placement) after the slanting Gobelin stitches are completed and can be worked in the same or a contrasting color.

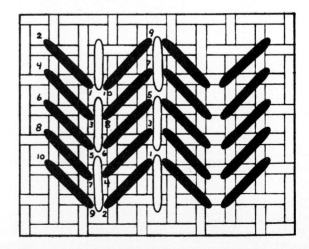

STEM, DIAGONAL

The sample is worked on #12 Zweigart® Mono canvas with DMC® Floralia® (3-ply Persian yarn).

This variation of the stem stitch is worked on the diagonal. In the diagram, I started with a compensating stitch (1-2).

Continue with vertical straight stitches over 2 horizontal canvas threads, dropping down 1 step for each stitch (3-4, 5-6, 7-8, etc.)

The return trip is worked as a horizontal stitch over 2 vertical canvas threads (11-12, 13-14, 15-16, etc.).

Repeat these 2 rows until the area to be stitched is covered.

Finally, using a darker color in a lighter-weight yarn, work a backstitch down the center of each double row (A-B, C-D, E-F, etc.).

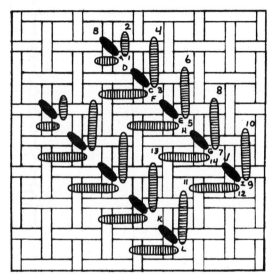

STEM VARIATION 1

The sample is worked on #10 Zweigart® Mono canvas with DMC® Floralia® (3-ply Persian yarn).

The Stem stitch is worked in vertical columns. It can be stitched in 1 or 2 colors. Always use a thinner yarn for the backstitches.

Start by working the diagonal stitches over 2 horizontal and 2 vertical canvas threads pointing left (1-2, 3-4, 5-6, etc.). Then, make the return trip pointing the diagonal stitch to the right (11-12, 13-14, 15-16, etc.).

Next, add the backstitch in a second color, using a lighter-weight yarn (A-B, C-D, E-F, etc.).

If desired, another row of backstitch can be placed between the vertical columns in a third color.

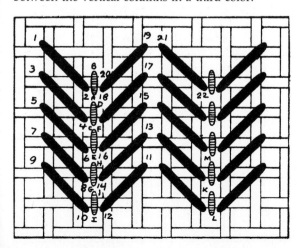

ST. GEORGE AND ST. ANDREW CROSS

The sample is worked on #10 Zweigart® Mono canvas with Anchor® Tapisserie (tapestry yarn).

The stitch is a combination of the Cross-Stitch (page 45) and the Upright Cross (page 50) placed alternately across the row. Each stitch is worked over 2 horizontal and 2 vertical canvas threads and can be worked horizontally, vertically, or diagonally, in 1 or 2 colors. If you decide to work this stitch in 2 colors, always complete either the cross-stitches or the upright crosses before starting the other. (See diagram.)

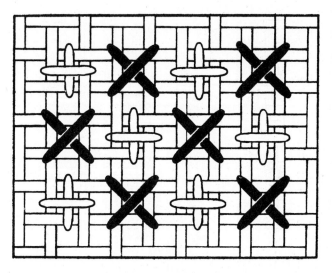

STRAIGHT AND UPRIGHT CROSSES, LARGE

The sample is worked on #14 Zweigart® Mono canvas with DMC® Floralia® (3-ply Persian yarn).

This is a combination of large cross-stitches worked over 4 horizontal and 4 vertical canvas threads and upright cross-stitches placed between them over 2 horizontal and 2 vertical canvas threads. (See diagram.)

The combination looks best when worked in 2 colors as shown in the sample.

SURREY

The sample is worked on #14 Zweigart® Mono canvas with DMC® Floralia® (3-ply Persian yarn).

The Surrey stitch is a looped stitch worked from left to right and from the bottom up to the top of the canvas. The stitch is worked over 2 horizontal and 2 vertical canvas threads.

To work the stitch, insert the needle into the canvas from the front at **1**, under 2 horizontal canvas threads, and out at **2**, leaving a tail that is held in place with your thumb (Diagram A). Insert the needle 2 threads to the right under 2 vertical canvas threads (**3-4**). The yarn is placed upward as shown in Diagram B.

The second stitch is started 2 vertical canvas threads to the right in the same hole as the start of the last diagonal stitch (**2-3**). See Diagram C.

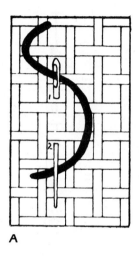 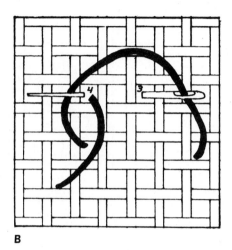 

A   B   C

T

TENT, ALTERNATING

The sample is worked on #10 Zweigart® Mono canvas with DMC® Floralia® (3-ply Persian yarn).

Work the Alternating Tent stitch in horizontal rows, changing the direction of the tent stitch every other stitch (**1-2, 3-4,** etc.).

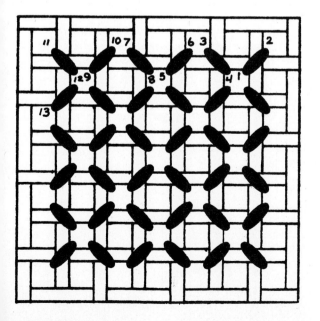 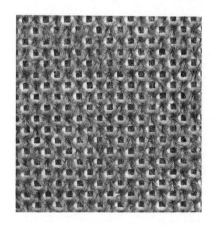

TENT, BASKETWEAVE
(basketweave)

The sample is worked on #10 Zweigart® Mono canvas with Anchor® Tapisserie (tapestry yarn).

The Basketweave Tent stitch is usually the "chosen" tent stitch for experienced stitchers. It gives the best front and back canvas coverage and does not distort the canvas as the Continental and the Half-Cross will.

The backing gives a woven appearance and is the first choice when the project will receive wear (chairs, cushions, etc.).

This stitch is worked in diagonal rows starting at the upper right-hand corner (**1-2**). Follow the numbering on the diagram and you will find a rhythm is quickly established.

Do not use a frame for this stitch.

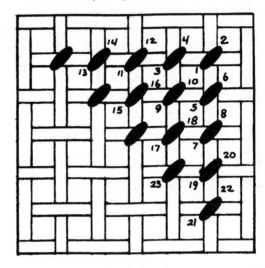

TENT, CONTINENTAL
(continental)

The sample is worked on #12 Zweigart® Mono canvas with Anchor® Tapisserie (tapestry yarn).

The Continental Tent stitch is the most popular of the tent stitches for beginner to intermediate stitchers.

Working horizontally across the row from right to left, follow the numbering on the diagram (**1-2, 3-4, 5-6, 7-8,** etc.). (See Diagram A.)

A vertical row of stitches is worked from top to bottom (**1-2, 3-4, 5-6,** etc.), turning the canvas as shown for the return trip. (See Diagram B.)

The back of the canvas looks like long slanted stitches.

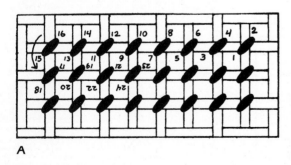

A

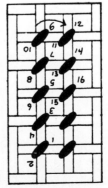

B

TENT, HALF-CROSS
(half-cross)

The sample is worked on #14 Zweigart® Penelope canvas with DMC® Floralia® (3-ply Persian yarn).

The Half-Cross Tent stitch gives the worst front and back coverage of all the tent stitches.

It should be worked on Penelope canvas. If it is worked on Mono canvas, the stitches will not be well formed. The rows will look ridged or ribbed in appearance.

The back of the canvas looks like vertical upright stitches and is considered a poor backing for a project subject to wear and tear. (See Diagram A.)

To stitch in vertical rows, follow Diagram B (1-2, 3-4, etc.), working from the top to the bottom of the row.

This stitch uses less yarn than any other tent stitch.

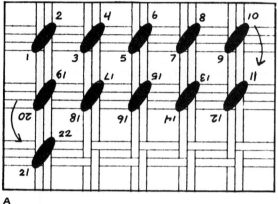

A

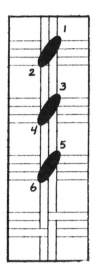

B

TENT VARIATION
(T-stitch)

The sample is worked on #14 Zweigart® Mono canvas with DMC® Floralia® (3-ply Persian yarn).

This tent stitch variation is an *exposed* stitch, so be very careful to follow the numbering on the diagram *exactly*, working each stitch in the direction of the arrows.

It is worked in a diagonal basketweave pattern over the intersection of 1 horizontal and 1 vertical canvas thread.

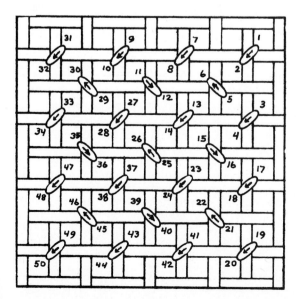

145

TIED DIAMONDS
(diamond with backstitch, roman filling

The sample is worked on #12 Zweigart® Mono canvas with Anchor® Tapisserie (tapestry yarn).

First, work an upright stitch over 2 horizontal canvas threads (**1-2**). Then, tie it down in the middle over 1 vertical canvas thread with a backstitch (**3-4**). Next, work an upright stitch over 4 horizontal canvas threads and tie it down in the middle with a backstitch. Continue in this way, working the stitches over 6, 8, 6, 4, and 2 horizontal canvas threads until a diamond shape is completed. Repeat these diamonds across the row.

The next row of tied diamonds is fitted in the diamond shape spaces of the row above, with the longest stitch fitted into the space between the diamonds. (See diagram.)

An alternate method: Work all upright stitches, then work backstitches across the row in the middle of the diamond.

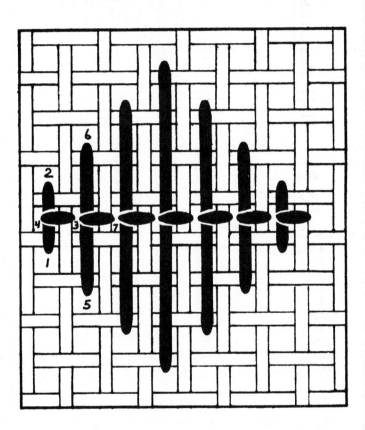

TIED STAR

The sample is worked on #14 Zweigart® Mono canvas with DMC® Floralia® (3-ply Persian yarn).

This stitch is worked in 3 shades or colors in stepped diagonal rows.

Start by working a diagonal stitch over 5 horizontal and 5 vertical canvas threads (**1-2**). Cross this with a diagonal stitch over 3 horizontal and 7 vertical canvas threads (**3-4**). Then, cross both stitches with a diagonal stitch over 7 horizontal and 3 vertical canvas threads (**5-6**). Finally, work a small tie stitch over the entire cross (**7-8**). Repeat for each stitch.

Change color for the next row (**A-B, C-D, E-F,** etc.).

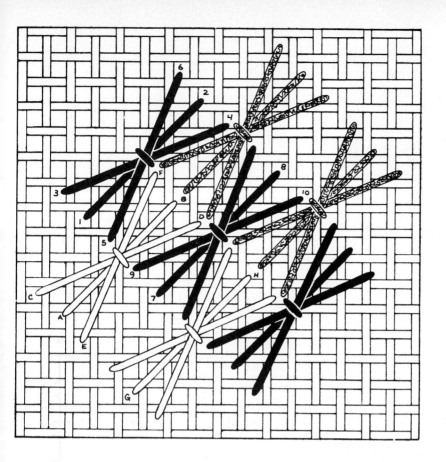

TRIANGLE

The sample is worked on #14 Zweigart® Mono canvas with Anchor® Tapisserie (tapestry yarn).

This is a decorative combination of different-size Gobelin stitches that form 4 triangle units into a square shape.

Each triangle unit is made of 7 Gobelin stitches. The first stitch is worked over 2 horizontal canvas threads, the second over 3, the third over 4, the fourth over 5, the fifth over 4, the sixth over 3, and the seventh over 2 canvas threads.

Rotate the canvas one-quarter turn and repeat for the second triangle. When the 4 triangle units are complete, add a cross-stitch in each corner to cover the exposed canvas and finish the square.

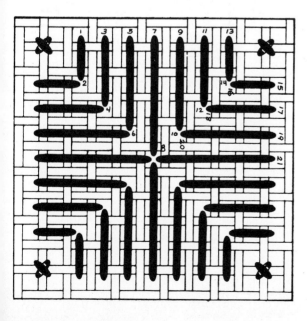

TRIPLE CROSS

The sample is worked on #10 Zweigart® Mono canvas with DMC® Floralia® (3-ply Persian yarn).

The Triple Cross-Stitch is worked over 3 horizontal and 3 vertical canvas threads. It is composed of 1 horizontal oblong cross-stitch (**1-2, 3-4**) over 1 horizontal and 3 vertical canvas threads and 1 vertical oblong cross-stitch (**5-6, 7-8**) over 3 horizontal and 1 vertical canvas thread.

Next, place a cross-stitch on top of these stitches (**9-10, 11-12**) over 3 horizontal and 3 vertical canvas threads.

This stitch may be used as an individual motif, grouped as a pattern, or as an allover background stitch.

TRIPLE TWIST

The sample is worked on Zweigart® Congress cloth with Anchor® floss.

The Triple Twist is an open stitch that leaves canvas threads exposed. It can be worked in horizontal or vertical rows or on the diagonal, as shown in the diagram.

First, work an elongated cross-stitch over 8 horizontal and 4 vertical canvas threads (**1-2, 3-4**). Then, work a second cross on top of the first and 1 vertical canvas thread inside those of the first cross over 8 horizontal and 2 vertical canvas threads (**5-6, 7-8**). The third cross is worked on top of the first two crosses, over 6 horizontal and 4 vertical canvas threads and 1 horizontal thread below and above the corners of the first cross (**9-10, 11-12**). See diagram.

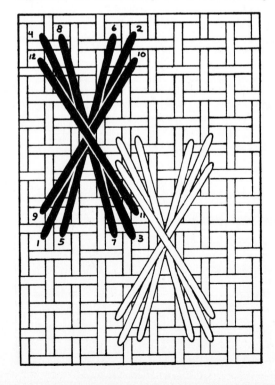

TUMBLING BLOCKS
(pavilion steps)

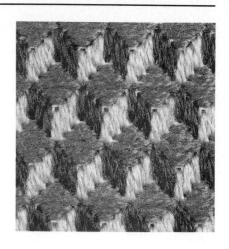

The sample is worked on #14 Zweigart® Mono canvas with DMC® Floralia® (3-ply Persian yarn).

This stitch is always worked in 3 colors or 3 shades of the same color. The completed pattern resembles a series of three-dimensional blocks or prisms and is very close in appearance to the Tumbling Blocks or Baby Blocks quilt pattern.

Work each color in horizontal rows stepped up or down as shown in the diagram.

Start with the darkest color, working over 4 horizontal canvas threads (**1-2, 3-4, 5-6,** etc.). Next, fill in the spaces with the lightest color (**A-B, C-D, E-F,** etc.).

Finish the row with the medium color worked in horizontal stitches over 2, 4, 6, 4, and 2 vertical canvas threads placed between the vertical stitches (**a-b, c-d, e-f,** etc.).

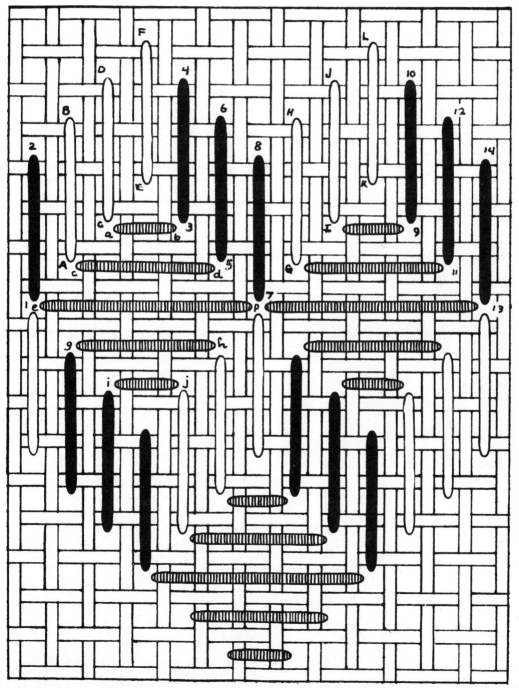

TURKEY
(Ghiordes knot, turkey knot, turkey tufting)

The sample is worked on #12 Zweigart® Mono canvas with DMC® Floralia® (3-ply Persian yarn).

This is the least complicated of all the looped stitches. It looks like rug hooking and can be used to simulate a carpet, animal fur, or hair. Each row is worked horizontally from left to right, from the *bottom* to the top.

Start by going in at **1** under 1 vertical canvas thread and coming up at **2**, leaving a 1" tail of yarn on the front of the canvas. Next, work a horizontal stitch over 2 vertical canvas threads going in at **3** and coming up at **4**, in the same hole as the start of the stitch. Now, while holding the loop (at the desired length) with your thumb, place the needle under the next vertical canvas thread to start the next stitch (**1-2**) on the diagram. Repeat to the end of the row and cut the yarn.

Start the next row with a new length of yarn at the left, leaving 1 or 2 horizontal canvas threads between rows. Begin 1 thread to the right of the first stitch, creating a staggered row of stitches. Do not cut the loops until all the stitches are complete.

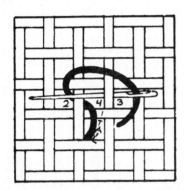
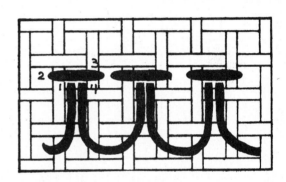

TURKISH, TWO-SIDED
(triangular, two-sided)

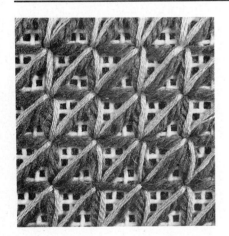

The sample is worked on #10 Zweigart® Mono canvas with Anchor® Tapisserie (tapestry yarn) and Anchor® floss.

This version of the Two-Sided Turkish stitch is worked horizontally in 1 or 2 colors.

Start by working upright vertical stitches across the row over 4 horizontal canvas threads, leaving 4 vertical canvas threads between the stitches (**1-2, 3-4, 5-6**).

Next, work a diagonal stitch over 4 horizontal and 4 vertical canvas threads (**7-8**) and a horizontal stitch over 4 vertical canvas threads (**9-10**). Repeat these 2 stitches across the row (**11-12, 13-14,** etc.). See Diagram A.

Finally, work the last part of the stitch in the same or an accent color (**A-B, C-D, E-F,** etc.). See Diagram B.

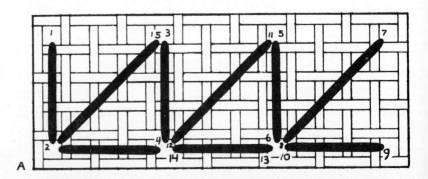

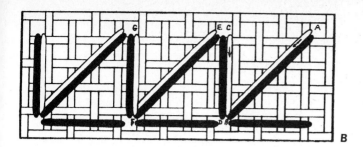

TWEED

The sample is worked on #10 Zweigart® Mono canvas with DMC® Floralia® (3-ply Persian yarn).

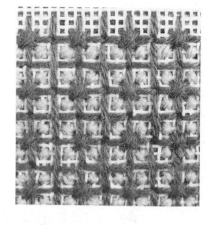

This stitch consists of large upright cross-stitches that are crossed in the center by a diagonal cross-stitch worked over 2 horizontal and 2 vertical canvas threads and smaller diagonal cross-stitches worked over 1 horizontal and 1 vertical canvas thread. Work in horizontal rows.

Start by making an upright cross-stitch over 6 vertical and 6 horizontal canvas threads (**1-2, 3-4**).

Next, work a diagonal cross-stitch in the center of the upright cross over 2 horizontal and 2 vertical canvas threads (**5-6, 7-8**). Repeat across the row.

Fit the second row of upright cross-stitches between the stitches of the first row (**A-B, C-D, E-F,** etc.).

Repeat these 2 rows across the area to be covered.

Finally, work a small diagonal cross-stitch over 1 horizontal and 1 vertical canvas thread in the center of the spaces left between the large upright crosses (**a-b, c-d, e-f,** etc.) in another shade to create a tweed effect.

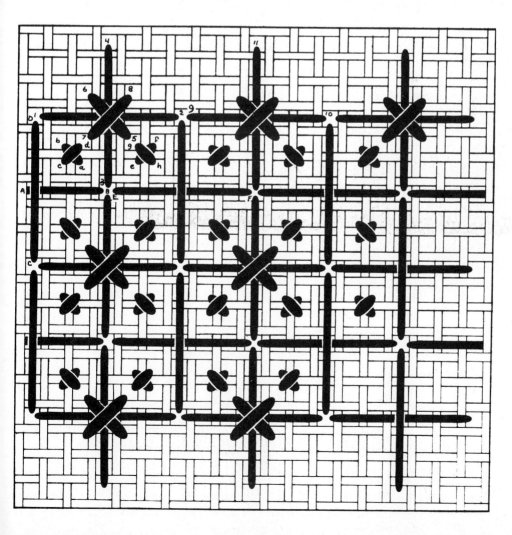

V

VANDYKE

The sample is worked on #14 Zweigart® Mono canvas with DMC® Floralia® (3-ply Persian yarn).

The Vandyke stitch is worked in vertical rows and forms a woven or braided pattern.

The stitch is an elongated cross worked over 3–4 horizontal and 2 vertical canvas threads. Each new stitch is placed over 1 canvas thread of the previous stitch.

It can be worked in 2 or more colors to produce a striped effect. This stitch makes a good border or background stitch.

VELVET

The sample is worked on #10 Zweigart® Mono canvas with DMC® Floralia® (3-ply Persian yarn).

This is a looped stitch that may also be cut to make a fringe or pile to resemble hair, carpet, or animal fur. It is worked over 2 horizontal and 2 vertical canvas threads.

First, make a half-cross stitch (**1-2**). Bring the needle out to the front at **3** and down at **4**, forming a loop on the front. Hold this loop with your thumb while you bring the needle forward to the front of the canvas under 2 horizontal canvas threads at **5** (Diagram A). Bring the yarn over the loop and work the top half of the cross-stitch by returning the needle to the back at **6**.

The next stitch begins in the same hole as the start of the top cross-stitch (**5**) and becomes **1** of the next stitch (Diagram B).

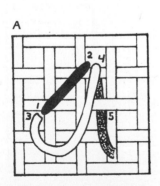

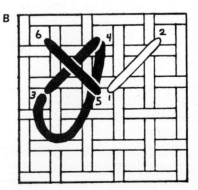

VICTORIAN, STEPPED

The sample is worked on #10 Zweigart® Mono canvas with DMC® Floralia® (3-ply Persian yarn).

This stitch consists of straight stitches worked right to left in a stepped pattern.

Use alternate colors or yarns for each row.

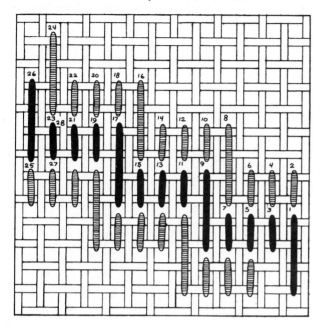

W

WAFFLE
(Norwich)

The sample is worked on #14 Zweigart® Mono canvas with DMC® Floralia® (3-ply Persian yarn).

The Waffle stitch can be worked over any *odd* number of canvas threads and can be used as an individual motif or an allover pattern. It is most attractive when worked with a tapestry yarn, silk, or cotton floss. The sample was worked over 9 horizontal and 9 vertical canvas threads.

Follow the diagram numbers closely to establish a regular pattern.

WEB

The sample is worked on #14 Zweigart® Mono canvas with DMC® Floralia® (3-ply Persian yarn).

This stitch resembles many Bokhara Couching stitches (pages 31–32) worked on the diagonal. It gives a close woven appearance.

To start, following the diagram, lay the thread across the canvas diagonally from **A** to **B**, **C** to **D**, etc., then tie this thread down, working the small tent stitches in the same or another color as shown on the diagram.

This stitch is tedious and slow to work. It is not recommended for large areas.

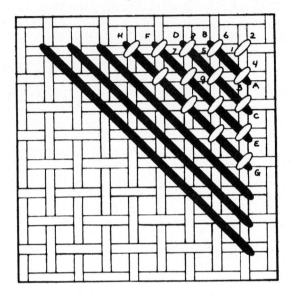

WHEATSHEAF
(sheaf, shell, wheat)

The sample is worked on #10 Zweigart® Mono canvas with DMC® Floralia® (3-ply Persian yarn).

This simpler version of the Shell stitch (page 134) is made of 3 upright straight stitches worked over any even number of horizontal canvas threads.

First, work the 3 upright straight stitches. Then, bring the needle up from the back in the center hole, but to the left of the upright straight stitches. Bring the yarn over these 3 stitches and back down into the same hole. This will cinch the stitches at the center.

To work this stitch over an odd number of horizontal canvas threads, the center tie stitch must be worked as a tent stitch over 1 horizontal and 1 vertical canvas thread.

WICKER

The sample is worked on #14 Zweigart® Mono canvas with DMC® Floralia® (3-ply Persian yarn).

This stitch resembles wicker when worked in 2 colors.

First, stitch the long vertical stitches (**1-2, 3-4, 5-6, 7-8**), over 6, 10, 10, and 6 horizontal canvas threads. Skip 3 vertical canvas threads and repeat across the row.

Next, fill in the spaces with 2 vertical stitches over 2 horizontal canvas threads (**a-b, c-d, e-f,** etc.), using the same color.

Finally, place the long horizontal stitch across the center of the vertical stitches covering 5 vertical canvas threads, using a darker shade (**A-B, C-D,** etc.).

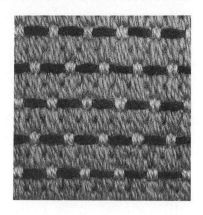

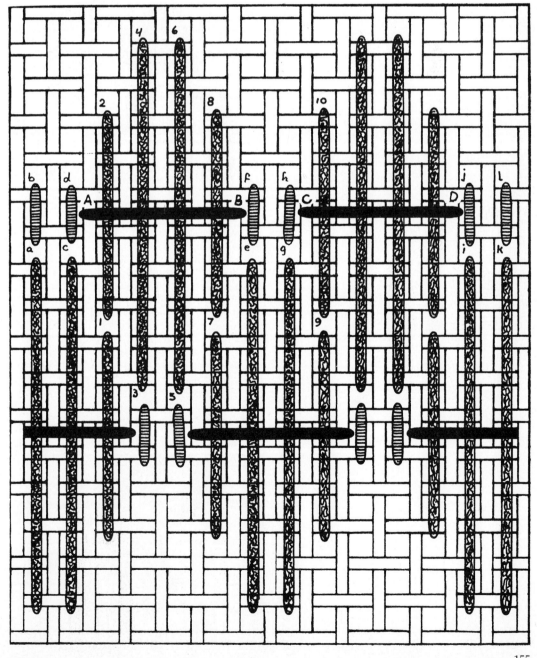

WINDMILL

The sample is worked on #10 Zweigart® Mono canvas with DMC® Floralia® (3-ply Persian yarn).

This stitch is worked as a surface motif on any small background stitch (tent, cross, etc.).

Start with a vertical straight stitch over 6 horizontal canvas threads (1-2). Next, work an elongated cross over this stitch (3-4, 5-6).

Make a horizontal straight stitch across the center of the stitches just completed (7-8) and an elongated cross over this stitch (9-10, 11-12).

WINDMILL, CROSS TIED

The sample is worked on #10 Zweigart® Mono canvas with DMC® Floralia® (3-ply Persian yarn) and DMC® #3 perle cotton.

This stitch is worked as a surface motif on any small background stitch (tent, cross, etc.).

Start by working a vertical straight stitch over 8 horizontal canvas threads (1-2). Next, make an elongated cross-stitch over 6 horizontal canvas threads, crossing the first stitch (3-4, 5-6). Then, work a horizontal straight stitch across the center of the stitches just completed (7-8). Add an elongated cross over it as worked on the first half of the stitch. Finally, work a small cross-stitch over the center of the stitches just worked.

WOVEN CROSS, ASKEW

The sample is worked on #12 Zweigart® Mono canvas with DMC® Floralia® (3-ply Persian yarn).

This stitch is worked in horizontal rows across the area to be covered.

Start with a cross over 4 horizontal and 4 vertical canvas threads (**1-2, 3-4**). Then, following the numbers on the diagram *exactly*, work the rest of the stitches (**5-6, 7-8,** etc.).

Note: Stitch **15-16** is worked *under* stitch **9-10**.

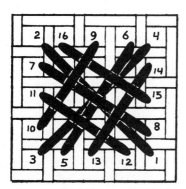

WOVEN RIBBONS

The sample is worked on Zweigart® Congress cloth with Anchor® floss.

This is a large filling stitch worked in graduating straight stitches, forming diagonal rectangles. The compensating stitches are worked in later in a second color as shown in the diagram (**A-B, C-D, E-F,** etc.).

Start by working a straight stitch over 2 horizontal canvas threads (**1-2**). Work a second straight stitch over 4 horizontal canvas threads (**3-4**), a third over 6 (**5-6**), etc. Continue following the diagram until the rectangle is completed.

Start the second rectangle 4 horizontal and 2 vertical canvas threads from the last stitch.

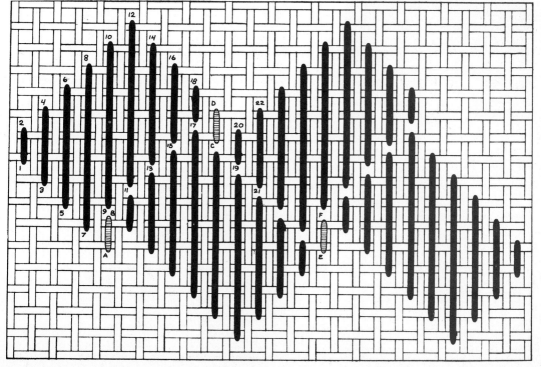

WOVEN SQUARE

The sample is worked on #14 Zweigart® Mono canvas with DMC® Floralia® (3-ply Persian yarn).

The Woven Square is worked in blocks cornered by a cross-stitch.

Start by stitching a block of 3 horizontal stitches across 4 vertical canvas threads (**1-2, 3-4, 5-6**).

Next, using the same or a lighter color, come up from the back at **A**, weave under **1-2**, over **3-4**, and under **5-6**, returning to the back at **B**. Begin the next stitch at **C**, weave over **1-2**, under **3-4**, and over **5-6**. The third stitch is a repeat of the first.

Finally, add the cross-stitches over 2 horizontal and 2 vertical canvas threads.

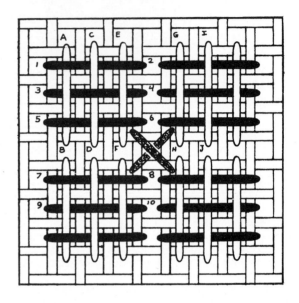

WOVEN TENT

The sample is worked on #10 Zweigart® Mono canvas with DMC® Floralia® (3-ply Persian yarn).

First, work a square of tent stitches over 4 horizontal and 4 vertical canvas threads (16 tent stitches).

Then, work 2 straight stitches: the first an upright stitch along the right side of the square over 4 horizontal canvas threads (**1-2**), and the second a horizontal stitch over 4 vertical canvas threads (**3-4**) placed across the bottom.

Next, weave the yarn *over* these 2 long stitches, covering the tent stitches as shown in the diagram.

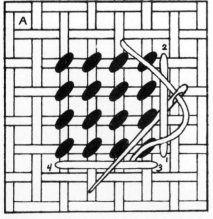

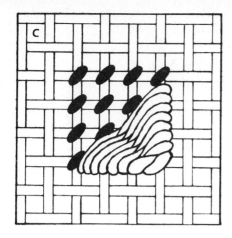

WOVEN TRELLIS

The sample is worked on #14 Zweigart® Mono canvas with DMC® Floralia® (3-ply Persian yarn).

This stitch can be worked over a square of 6–10 horizontal and vertical canvas threads.

Start at any corner and work 1 stitch from the outside to the center hole. Then, place a stitch 1 canvas thread away on each side of this stitch, forming a unit of 3 stitches. Repeat these 3 stitches in each corner.

Bring the yarn up from the back into the center hole and weave (as shown in the diagram) over and under the 3 stitches until they are covered completely. Repeat for each of the other 3 units.

This stitch will leave the canvas threads exposed.

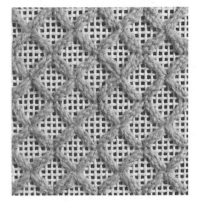

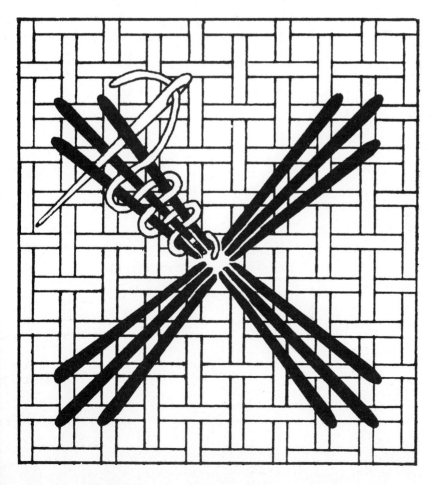

Z

ZIGZAG
(stepped backstitch, steps)

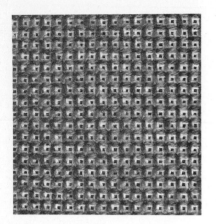

The sample is worked on #14 Zweigart® Mono canvas with DMC® Floralia® (3-ply Persian yarn).

This easy little stitch is made of a series of backstitches worked over 2 canvas threads, forming a stepped zigzag pattern. It is worked on the diagonal starting at the lower left and ending at the upper right.

First, work a vertical backstitch over 2 horizontal canvas threads (**1-2**), then a horizontal backstitch over 2 vertical canvas threads (**3-4**). Repeat these 2 stitches diagonally across the area to be covered.

The second or return row is worked in a lighter shade of the same color, starting at the top and going in a downward direction.

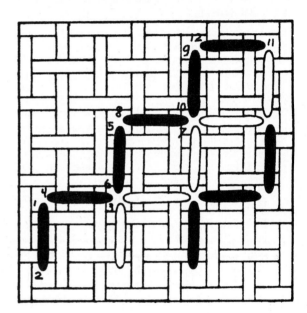

Projects

BELT

This is the easiest needlepoint project to work for the beginner or the needleworker looking for a simple project to carry and stitch when waiting for appointments, etc.

Materials

#10 plastic canvas 12 threads high by waist measurement plus 6". This project can also be worked on #10 Mono canvas.
#18 tapestry needle
Yarn DMC® Floralia® 3-ply Persian in 2 contrasting colors:
  Blanc (white)—3 skeins
  Noir (black)—4 skeins
Military-type buckle

Preparation

To determine the length of the canvas, measure your waist and add 6". Make a mark 6" from one end for the tongue of the belt. Then fold the canvas in half to this mark to find the center.

Stitching

Following the diagram for color and design placement, begin stitching at the center mark using 3-ply Persian yarn and the Continental stitch (page 144). Leave 1 canvas thread at the top and bottom of the buckle end and 2 canvas threads at the tongue end unworked for finishing later with the binding stitch.

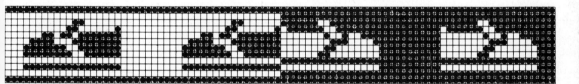

Finishing

Using the darker color, work the Binding Stitch (page 11) around the perimeter over the canvas threads left unworked.

Attach the buckle and the belt is finished. If you want to cover the back of the work, line the belt with a length of ribbon cut to the size of the canvas. The ribbon can be glued or slip-stitched to the binding stitch.

See color photograph.

CAMERA CASE WITH STRAP

Since cameras are made in many sizes, I have designed a basic box-shape case that can hold a small camera or film, lenses, filters, and other small accessories.

The strap can also be made as a separate piece that can be attached to an existing camera using two swivel snaps, available in craft and leathercraft stores.

Materials

#10 plastic canvas cut as follows:
- Bottom: 1 piece 55 threads × 35 threads
- Sides: 2 pieces 33 threads × 43 threads
- Front/Back: 2 pieces 55 threads × 33 threads
- Top: 1 piece 57 threads × 32 threads
- Front lip: 1 piece 5 threads × 57 threads
- Strap: 1 piece 18 threads high × 348 threads long. The length can be adjusted to fit your own size.

#20 tapestry needle

Yarn DMC® Floralia® 3-ply Persian:
- Black—75 yards
- Dark gray—5 yards
- Light gray—40 yards
- Blue—60 yards

2 "D" rings

2 Velcro® dots ⅜" diameter

Corrugated cardboard (cut from an old carton) 3½" × 16", used to stiffen the inside of the box

Felt for lining 3½" × 16"

Preparation

Cut the plastic canvas to the sizes given. Using the horizontal stripe alphabet (page 192), prepare your chosen monogram. *Note:* The camera motif is overlaid on the right-hand letter of the monogram.

Stitching

Follow the design chart, stitch each piece using 2-ply yarn. Be sure to leave the indicated number of threads unworked for binding and joining as shown on the chart. The bottom piece is stitched leaving 1 thread unworked around the perimeter for later joining.

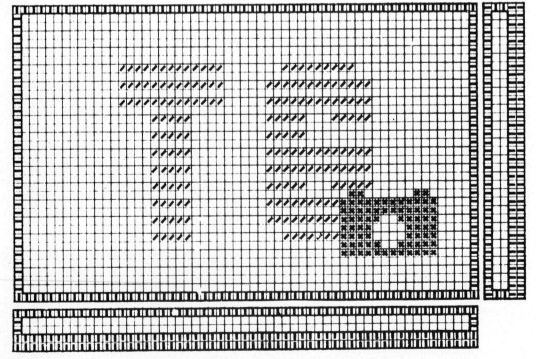

Top

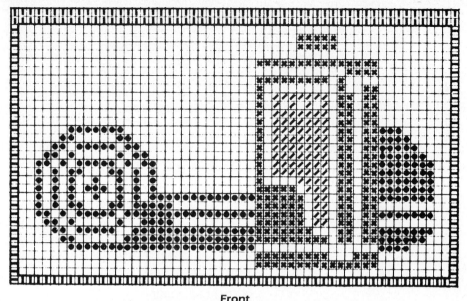

Front

Bottom

Sides ②

Strap

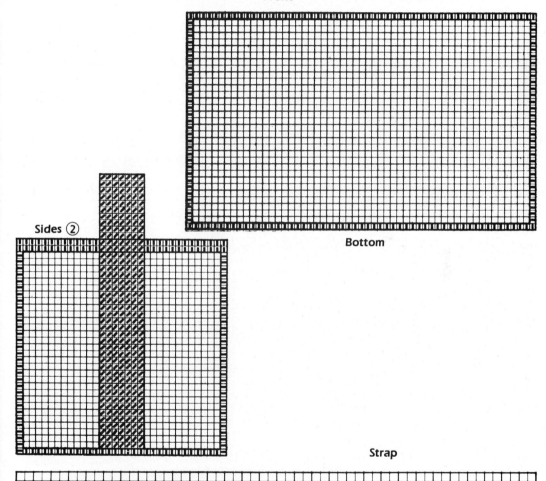

Finishing

All binding and joining edges are worked in black yarn. Bind the edges of the side tabs and slip them through the "D" rings. Fold them to the inside and stitch in place.

Join the front, back, and side pieces to the bottom using the Binding Stitch (page 11). Join the corners and bind the top edges of the sides and front.

Join the lip to the front edge of the top piece. Then join the back of the top piece to the top of the back piece. Bind all unworked edges of the top.

To finish the neck strap, bind all unworked edges. Next, slip the strap tab through the "D" ring on the box, folding it to the back of the neck strap. Stitch across.

Cut the felt and cardboard into 5 pieces each, to fit the bottom, sides (2), front, and back. Glue the felt to the cardboard, insert into the box, and glue to the needlework.

Attach the Velcro® dots to the lip and top edge of the front for a neat closure.

Stitched by Teresa Gustafson.

See color photograph.

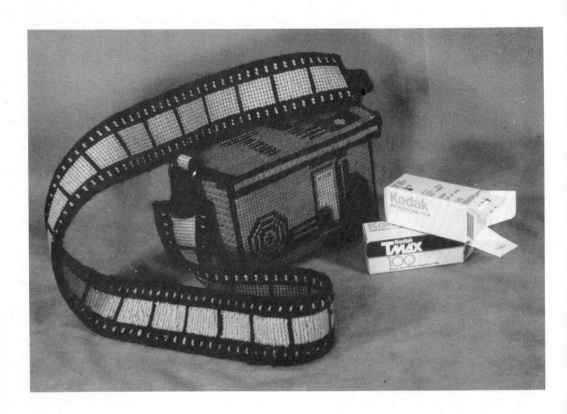

DALE'S STITCHING LADY

This picture was generously loaned to me by Dale Sokolow to show that the proper placement of different stitches and fibers and the combination of various mesh canvases appliquéd together can produce a truly spectacular piece of needlework.

Dale designed and made her "Stitching Lady" for Step 6 of the Embroiderers' Guild of America Master Craftsman Program in canvas stitchery.

For this project, Dale used the following stitches:

Window frame—Split Gobelin

Shawl—Diagonal knitting

Fringe—Velvet Stitch

Chair wood—Knotted Stitch

Window shades—Blackwork Pattern

Window shade outside—Couching

Chair—Pavilion Diamonds

Chair arms—Tent and Diagonal Gobelin

Footstool—French Knots

Skirt bottom—Diagonal Gobelin

Floor—Brick

Lace around neck—Detached Buttonhole

See color photograph.

Dress top—Byzantine

Dress bottom—Byzantine and Tent

Tablecloth—Bargello Pattern and Whipped Outline Stitch

Oval picture on wall—Tent Stitch on #40 Silk Gauze

Raindrops on window—Diagonal Stitch

Wallpaper—Diaper Pattern

Chair—Gobelin or Satin

Toss pillow—Bargello Pattern

Footstool legs—Split Stitch

Base molding—Diagonal Satin

Lamp—Encroaching Gobelin, Split Stitch, Whipped Outline

Face and hands—on #30 Silk Gauze Basketweave Stitch

EYEGLASS CASE

Nothing looks as pretty as taking your glasses or sunglasses out of an elegant eyeglass case. This sample was made for "dressy wear" by using 3 metallic braid threads as an accent.

Materials

#18 Zweigart® Mono canvas 10″ × 11″
#24 tapestry needle
Yarn Anchor® floss
   Black—4 skeins used 5-ply
   Turquoise—2 skeins used 5-ply
Kreinik #16 medium braid—Gold and 2 multicolor reels
Lining Black satin 7″ × 8″

Preparation

Work this project on a frame to avoid distortion. Choose your initials from the vertical stripe alphabet (page 191) and place on the diagram (in lieu of JG).

Following the diagram, stitch the 3 rows of Upright Gobelin (page 79) using the 3 metallic braid threads. Next, work the initials in Continental stitch (page 144) and fill in the background around the initials with Basketweave stitch (page 144) in 5-ply floss. Work the bottom half of the metallic braid threads as shown on the diagram. Notice that a heart shape is formed around the initials. Continue working the Gobelin stitch over 4 horizontal canvas threads for 9 rows, following the shape of the bottom of the heart, using 5-ply black floss.

Fill in the top and bottom borders in Diagonal Mosaic stitch (page 105) using 5-ply black floss.

Finishing

Block if necessary (see "Blocking," page 190). Cut around the needlework, leaving ½″ of unworked canvas threads. Fold the unworked canvas to the back, leaving 2 threads at the top and 1 thread at the sides and bottom for binding and joining. Press or baste in place.

Fold the canvas in half lengthwise. Using the Binding Stitch (page 11), join the edges starting at the top and working downward around the bottom.

Work the binding stitch over the 2 unworked canvas threads around the top edge.

Fold the lining in half lengthwise and stitch around 1 long and 1 short side (½″ seam allowance). Slip the lining into the case and fold the top edge to the back to fit. Slip-stitch to the top edge.

See color photograph.

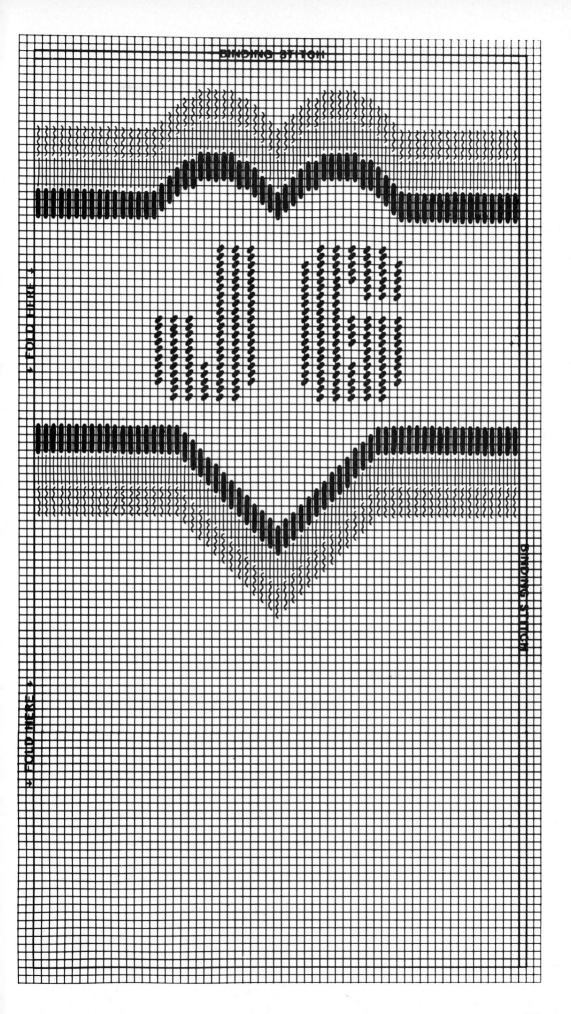

FIRST AID BOX

The First Aid Box is intended for use on a boat, at your pool, or in the well-decorated bathroom. This is a project that will be used by the entire family.

Materials

#10 plastic canvas cut as follows:
Top: 1 piece 129 threads × 129 threads, 4 pieces 10 threads × 129 threads
Bottom: 1 piece 119 threads × 119 threads, 4 pieces 119 threads × 30 threads
Heavy cardboard   Same sizes as the canvas
#20 tapestry needle
Yarn   DMC® Floralia® 3-ply Persian:
Lid: Navy blue—50 yards, Red—80 yards, White—40 yards
Bottom: Navy blue—150 yards

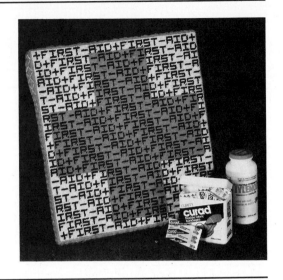

Preparation

Cut the canvas to the *exact* thread count given for the 5 top pieces and the bottom 5 pieces.

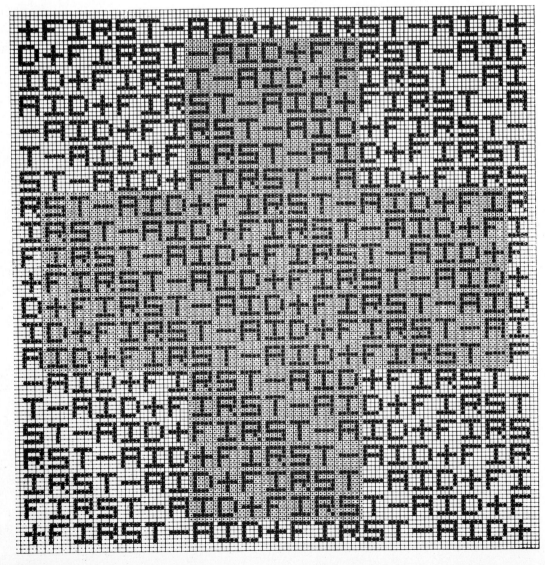

Stitching

Following the design diagram, using the Half-Cross (page 145) or Continental stitch (page 144) and 3-ply yarn, stitch each piece. Leave 1 canvas thread unworked around the perimeter of each piece for joining and binding.

The sample was stitched using the following stitches:

Top of box—Continental
Sides of the top—Diamond eyelet
Box bottom—Diamond eyelet or Continental
Sides of box bottom—Encroaching Gobelin

Finishing

Join the 1" sides to the top of the box using the Binding Stitch (page 11) over the 1 canvas thread left unworked. Next, join the four corners.

Join the 3" sides to the box bottom in the same way, joining the corners as you work. Finally, bind all the unworked edges of the box bottom and top.

Cut heavy cardboard to fit as a stiffener for each piece and glue to the inner surfaces.

Stitched by Kathleen Wolter.

See color photograph.

FLASK COVER

This is designed for the well-dressed spectator at the football game.

Materials

#10 plastic canvas   43 threads × 103 threads for the flask shown. For a different shape or size flask, measure the circumference around the middle and multiply by 10 threads per inch. Add 5 threads to compensate for the bulk of the yarn.
#20 tapestry needle
Yarn   DMC® Floralia® 3-ply Persian and Kreinik silver #32 heavy braid:
Initials—36 yards
Background—41 yards
Double-sided adhesive tape   4″ long

Preparation

Cut the plastic canvas to size. Measure and mark the center with a waterproof marking pen.
Choose your initials from the vertical stripe alphabet (page 191) and place it as shown on the diagram.

Stitching

First, stitch the monogram using the #32 heavy braid in silver. Stitch the background with 3-ply Persian yarn, leaving 2 threads unworked at the top and bottom along the long edges.
The sample was stitched using the Diagonal Mosaic stitch (page 105) for the background.

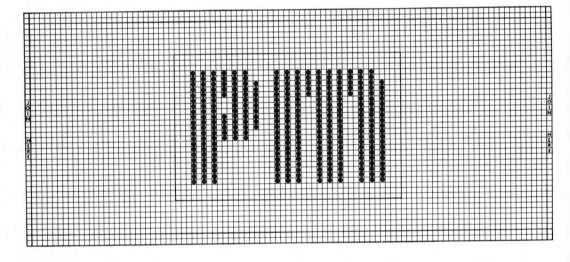

Finishing

When the stitching is completed, place the short edges side by side to form a tube. *Do not overlap.* Join the two short edges by continuing the Diagonal Mosaic stitch in the established pattern. Place the double-sided tape on the flask at the back seam line (vertically). Slip the needlepointed cover over the flask and press firmly on the taped line.
Stitched by Anita Miller.
See color photograph.

JEWELRY/TOOL CASE

This Jewelry/Tool Case was designed for the bicyclist who would never think of going anywhere without tools, but it can be made for jewelry or other items. As shown, it can be filled with tools and fit around the bar of a bicycle.

Materials

#12 Zweigart® Mono canvas   9½″ × 11″ (finished size is 6″ × 8″)
#20 tapestry needle
Yarn   DMC® Floralia® 3-ply Persian:
  Tan—6 skeins
  Black—2 skeins
Cording   1 yard black
Felt for lining   8″ × 10″
Felt for tool pocket (same as lining)   5″ × 9″
2 Velcro® dots   ½″ diameter

Preparation

Cut the canvas to the size specified and tape all around with masking tape to prevent raveling. Select your monogram letters from the vertical or horizontal stripe alphabets (pages 191–192).

Stitching

Follow the diagram for placement of bicycle motifs and initials and stitch using the Continental stitch (page 144) and 2-ply yarn. Remember to work on a frame when using any diagonal stitches to prevent distortion.

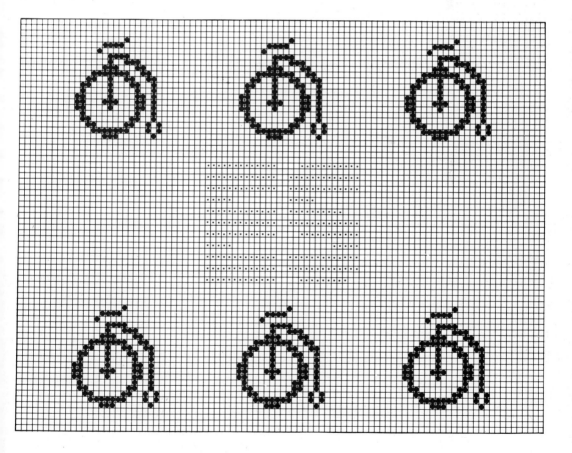

Finishing

Block the piece if necessary (see "Blocking," page 190). Trim the unworked canvas to 1" all around the stitched area.

Pin the cording all around the perimeter of the stitched area, cording in, and baste.

Fold 1 long edge of the pocket lining 1" to the back and pin. Stitch across ¼" from the top edge.

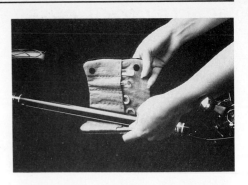

Place the pocket on top of the lining with both right sides facing up. Line up the bottom edges and mark the pocket according to the diagram. Stitch along these lines, going through both the pocket and the lining pieces. You will have 6 pockets, each 1" wide. If you are using the piece for jewelry, make three 2" pockets.

Place the lining and pocket assembly on the needlepoint, right sides facing. Stitch around the outside edge on the cording basting line. Leave about 4" open at the bottom edge for turning.

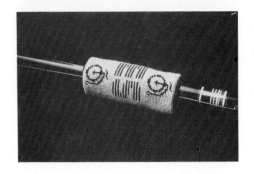

Turn to the right side and slip-stitch the opening closed.

Place half of 2 Velcro® dots on the top and bottom bicycles (upper and lower left-hand side) and the other half of the Velcro® dots on the inside as marked on the diagram.

Stitched by Liz Stewart Eanniccone.

See color photograph.

KEY CHAIN/IDENTIFICATION TAG

This project can be used as a key chain with a photograph or a luggage tag with your name and address in the space provided. It is a wonderful "quickie" project or stocking stuffer.

Materials

#10 plastic canvas 2 pieces 29 threads × 35 threads
#20 tapestry needle
Yarn Anchor® Tapisserie (tapestry yarn) or 6-strand Anchor® floss, doubled:
2 colors—1 skein each
Beaded key chain

Preparation

Cut canvas according to the chart (29 threads wide × 35 threads high). Following the front diagram, cut out the center of 1 piece, leaving 11 canvas threads at the top, bottom, and each side. Use a crafts knife to make a clean cut. This part will now look like a picture frame.

Choose a letter from the 5 × 5 alphabet (page 191) and an initial or motif for the back.

Stitching

Front: First, stitch the outline grid squares, leaving 2 canvas threads unworked around the outer edge and center cutout. Fill in the initial of your choice from the 5 × 5 alphabet in each square. Next, fill in the background using a contrasting color.

Back: Center a motif or stripe initial on the back. Fill in the background in the contrasting color, leaving 2 threads unworked around the outside.

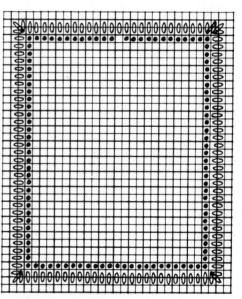

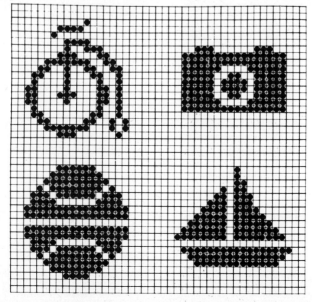

Motifs (for back)

Finishing

First, work the Binding Stitch (page 11) around the cutout of the front piece over the 2 unworked canvas threads.

Put the front and back sides together, wrong sides facing. Line up the unworked holes and proceed to join the two pieces using the binding stitch. Remember to leave 1 hole unworked for the chain.

Slip a paper ID or photograph into the opening in the front of the tag.

See color photograph.

LUGGAGE RACK

The Luggage Rack is a handsome addition to any guest room. It can also be used to hold a bedspread in your bedroom.

Materials

#10 Zweigart® Mono canvas   3 pieces 8″ × 24″
#18 tapestry needle
Yarn   DMC® Floralia® 3-ply Persian:
   Green, 4 shades—2 skeins each
   Yellow, 4 shades—2 skeins each
   Brown, 4 shades—2 skeins each
   Blue, 4 shades—2 skeins each
   Black—3 skeins
Felt for lining   3 pieces—5″ × 20″
Wood luggage rack

Preparation

Choose a Bargello pattern (see pages 16–22) that will fit the 3″ width of the canvas design area or use the chart in the diagram. Tape the canvas on all four sides to prevent raveling.

Stitching

Work the Bargello pattern according to the chart using 3-ply Persian yarn over 4 horizontal canvas threads. Continue the repeat of the pattern until the stitched canvas measures 19″.

Finishing

Block the needlepoint (see "Blocking," page 190). Fold 1″ of the felt lining to the back on each long side. Slip-stitch in place. Place the needlepoint on the right side of the felt and slip-stitch together. Lay the finished straps on top of the straps provided with the rack and tack or staple to the wood.

See color photograph.

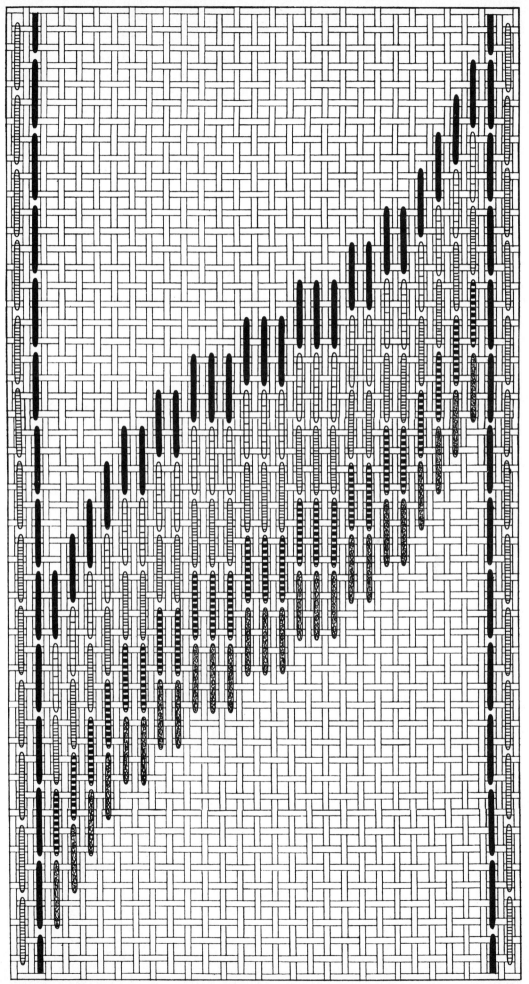

PICTURE OF GEORGE

This picture was included to show how a unique needlepoint portrait can be made without any artistic ability.

Materials

> **#14 Zweigart® Mono canvas** 14″ × 16″
> **#22 tapestry needle**
> **Yarn** DMC® Floralia® 3-ply Persian:
> Navy—30 yards
> Light blue—65 yards
> **Mounting board:**
> Prefinished wood—10″ × 13″
> ½″ half-round molding—40″
> **Or 8″ × 10″ frame**

Preparation

I took a snapshot of my husband to the photo store and asked them to make a "high-contrast" enlargement. A high-contrast photograph shows the black and white parts of a picture, with the grays dropping out completely.

Trace the outline of the dark areas and transfer this outline drawing (I used a waterproof marking pen and a light box) to the canvas.

Work this project on a frame to prevent distortion.

Stitching

Using 2-ply Persian yarn in the darker color, stitch the dark areas in the Continental stitch (page 144). Then, stitch the light areas of the figure in the same stitch using the light color yarn. Finally, stitch the background using the light color yarn in the Diagonal Mosaic stitch (page 105).

Finishing

If necessary, block the needlepoint picture (see "Blocking," page 190). Trim the unworked canvas threads to ½″ all around the picture.

Have the picture framed or tack it to a board as I did for the sample and cut the ½″ molding to fit over the unworked canvas threads.

See color photograph.

POCKET

This Pocket can be attached either to a jacket or to the outside of an athletic bag to hold small items.

Materials

> **#10 plastic canvas** 53 threads × 58 threads
> **#18 tapestry needle**
> **Yarn** DMC® Floralia® 3-ply Persian:
> Letter: Royal blue—10 yards
> Circle: Medium blue—1 yard
> Background: Light blue—16 yards
> Racquet: Silver—2 yards

Preparation

Cut the plastic canvas to the pocket shape using the diagram as a guide. Choose your letter (pages 191–192) and motif if desired, to replace the ones shown on the sample and chart.

Stitching

Using the Half-Cross (page 145) or the Continental stitch (page 144), follow the design chart, leaving 2 canvas threads all around the outer edge for finishing.

Finishing

Use the Binding Stitch (page 11) over 2 canvas threads to finish the outer edges of the pocket with the same yarn used for the background.

Pocket stitched by Anita Miller.
See color photograph.

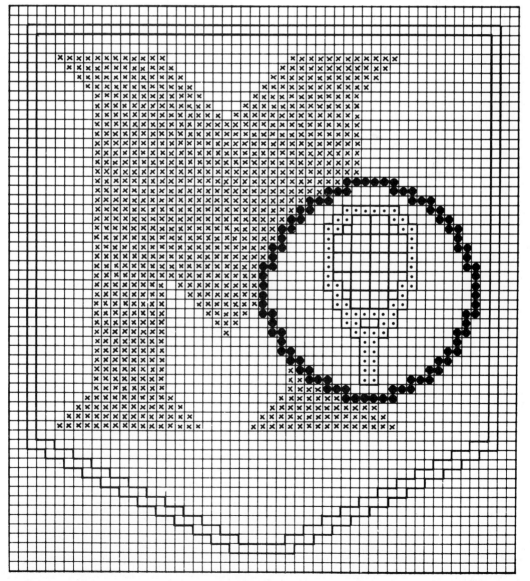

SNEAKER KEY/COIN HOLDER

Here is the perfect item for the athlete who would like to have his/her hands free, but needs to have a place to put a locker or house key and a little money. The sneaker wallet lets you have your hands free and your pockets empty.

Materials

> **#12 Zweigart Mono canvas** cut as follows:
> 1 piece 5″ × 11″
> 1 piece 3″ × 9½″
> **#20 tapestry needle**
> **Yarn** DMC® Floralia® 3-ply Persian:
> Color 1: Light—15 yards
> Color 2: Dark—11 yards
> **Lightweight felt for lining:**
> 1 piece 2″ × 2″
> 1 piece ¾″ × 4″
> **Velcro®** ¾″ × 5″

Preparation

To avoid severe distortion and extensive blocking, work all pieces on a frame. Place masking tape around the raw edges of the canvas to prevent raveling.

Mark the outline of the pieces to be stitched on the canvas using a waterproof marking pen. The larger piece is 24 canvas threads wide by 98 canvas threads long; the narrow piece is 9 canvas threads wide by 76 canvas threads long.

Stitching

Begin to stitch the larger piece at the upper right-hand corner using the darker color in the Basketweave stitch (page 144). The Basketweave stitch is recommended because it follow the natural flow of the rep-stripe pattern.

Do not stitch in the blank areas of the chart. Velcro® tape will be attached here during the finishing.

To work the narrow strip (fastening tab), stitch 3 vertical rows of color 1, 3 vertical rows of color 2, and 3 vertical rows of color 1.

Finishing

Block the stitched pieces (see "Blocking," page 190). If you stitched on a frame, the blocking should be minimal.

Separate the Velcro® into its two parts (rough and smooth). Cut the rough side in half, each piece measuring 2½″ long. Stitch these to the two areas left unstitched as marked on the diagram. Trim around the narrow strip, leaving 5 canvas threads all around the edge. Fold the unworked canvas to the back and press or baste in place. Cut the smooth side of the Velcro to 4″ and slip-stitch it to the back of this narrow strip (fastening tab). Trim around the larger needleworked piece and fold the unworked canvas to the back, leaving 2 canvas threads exposed on the front all around the perimeter. Press or baste in place.

Attach the fastening tab at the fold line as shown on the diagram.

Fold on the fold line, forming the pocket, and stitch the Binding Stitch (page 11), joining the canvas as you work around the entire perimeter.

Trim the 2″ piece of felt to fit inside the cover and slip-stitch in place.

See color photograph.

SODA/BEER CAN COVER

The can covers are both functional and decorative. Cold beverage cans "sweat" and wet both the hand and the table.

Materials

>   **#10 plastic canvas** cut as follows:
>   1 piece 28 threads × 90 threads
>   1 plastic canvas circle 3″ diameter cut to 2¾″
>   **#20 tapestry needle**
>   **Yarn**   Anchor® Tapisserie (tapestry)—approximately 40 yards

Preparation

Cut the plastic canvas to the size given (28 threads × 90 threads). The circle might be easiest cut from a purchased 3″-diameter circle. The two samples shown used the horizontal stripe alphabet (page 192) and the International Code of Signals flag alphabet. (See *The New Dictionary of Quilt Designs in Cross-stitch*, Crown, 1991).

Stitching

Center your monogram and start stitching 6 canvas threads from the top long edge. When the initials are finished, work the background in a lighter color.

Leave 2 canvas threads unworked at the top for the binding stitch and 1 canvas thread at the bottom and short sides for joining.

Use the Continental stitch (page 144) for this project.

Stitch the plastic circle using the darker color.

Finishing

Join the 2 short edges of canvas to form a tube. Work 1 vertical row of Continental stitch over both edges of the canvas. Next, place the stitched plastic circle (bottom) at the lower edge of the tube just formed and join with the Binding Stitch (page 11).

Finally, work a row of binding stitches around the top edge over the 2 unworked canvas threads.

See color photograph.

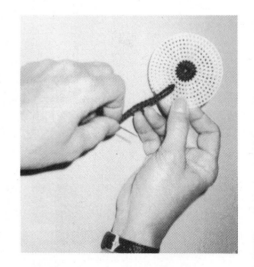

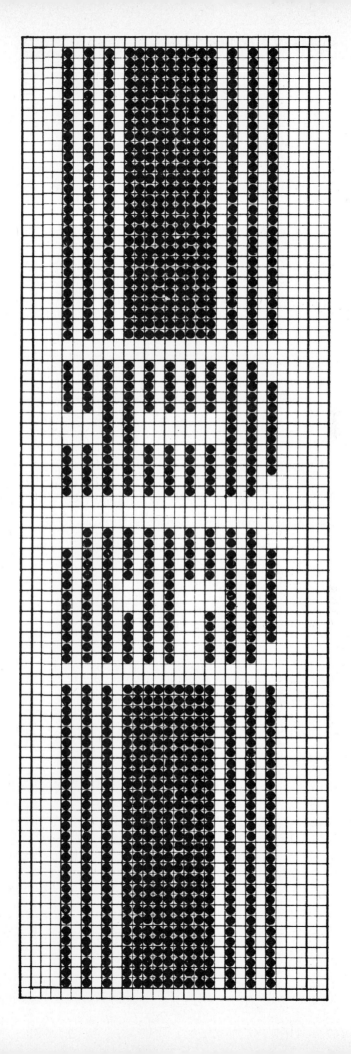

SQUASH OR BADMINTON RACQUET CASE

This case can be made to accommodate two squash racquets or up to four badminton racquets. This would be very sharp-looking at a tournament.

Materials

#7 plastic canvas cut as follows:
Bottom and top: 2 pieces 67 threads × 206 threads
Back: 1 piece 20 threads × 206 threads
Top side lips: 2 pieces 14 threads × 64 threads
Top front lip: 1 piece 14 threads × 206 threads
Bottom sides: 2 pieces 18 threads × 65 threads
Bottom front strip: 1 piece 14 threads × 206 threads
Handles: 2 pieces 8 threads × 98 threads
The finished size is 29½" × 9½" × 3".
#18 tapestry needle
Yarn DMC® Floralia® 3-ply Persian:
Red—47 skeins
Blue—76 skeins
Medium-weight cardboard for stiffening:
2 pieces 2½" × 29"
2 pieces 2½" × 9"
Felt for lining 1 yard 36" wide
Velcro® 1½" wide × 29" long, and 4 dots ¾" diameter

Preparation

Cut the canvas to the sizes given. Count carefully.
Choose your initials from the 5 × 5 alphabet (page 191). The large initial is optional.

Stitching

Stitch the 2 large top and bottom pieces according to the design diagram. Then, stitch the side strips using the Mosaic stitch (page 104) in the stripe pattern shown or solid throughout. Leave 1 thread unworked on all sides that join to other pieces. On edges that do not join, leave 2 canvas threads for the binding stitch.
Finally, stitch the handles, leaving 2 threads unworked on all edges. Work the Mosaic stitch over the 4 center threads.

Finishing

Join the four 3"-high side pieces to the bottom using the Binding Stitch (page 11). Join the corners with the same stitch.
Join the three 2"-high pieces to the top and join the corners.
Next, join the last edge of the top piece to the top of the 3"-high long side of the bottom.
Attach the handles as shown on the chart.
Cut the cardboard pieces. Glue one 2½" × 29" piece to the inside of the center back strip. Glue the other pieces in place in the same manner. Pockets may be added to hold the racquets in place.
Cut the felt lining and glue in place.
Attach Velcro® dots to the top and bottom front lip for a neat closure.
See color photograph.

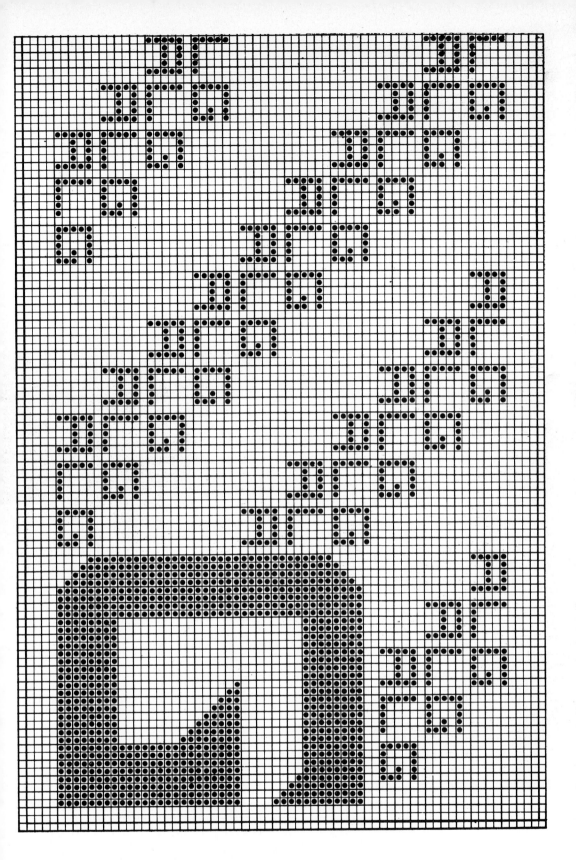

TENNIS RACQUET COVER

Every good tennis racquet needs a cover to dress it up.

Materials

#12 Zweigart® Interlock canvas The size of your racquet plus 3″ on all four sides
#20 tapestry needle
Yarn DMC® Floralia® 3-ply Persian:
  White—110 yards
  2 colors—1 skein each
  Kreinik #32 heavy braid:
  Silver—5½ yards (1 roll)
Plastic fabric or cotton duck for backing The size is determined by the size of your racquet.
Zipper The size is determined by the size of your racquet.
Cording Optional

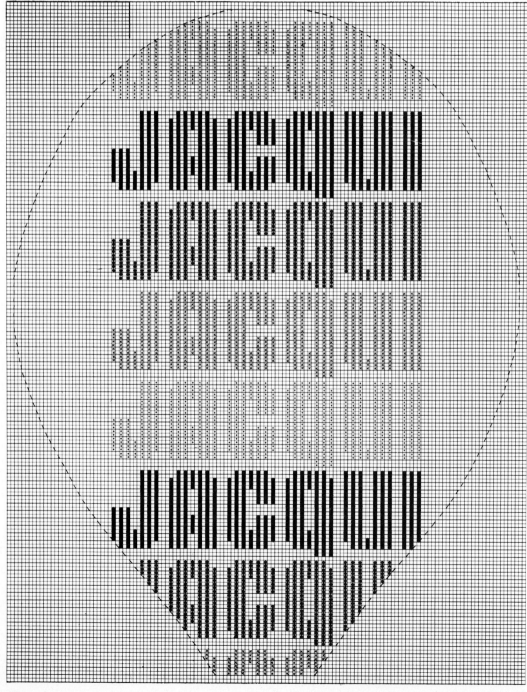

Preparation

Trace the shape of your racquet on a piece of paper, adding 1" all around the shape for the thickness of the racquet.

Using a waterproof marking pen, trace around your paper pattern on the center of the canvas. Work on a frame to minimize distortion.

Stitching

Follow the design chart for the placement of the letters (pages 191–192) in your name. Using the Continental stitch (page 144) and 2-ply yarn, work the name with the colors as follows: dark, medium, light, silver.

When the names are complete, work the background in white 2-ply yarn.

Finishing

If necessary, block the needlepointed canvas (see "Blocking," page 190). Cut around the shape of the needlepoint, leaving 1" of unworked canvas threads.

Cut the paper pattern you made in half lengthwise. Add 1" at the cut line and trace both halves onto the backing fabric. Cut out. Fold the 1" to the back and baste in place. Attach a zipper of the correct length according to the manufacturer's directions.

Baste the cording (if used) along the needlepointed edge facing in.

To assemble, place the canvas and backing together (right sides facing) and stitch (along the basting line of the cording, if used). Fold the bottom edge to the back and tack in place.

Stitched by Jacqui O'Connell.
See color photograph.

TENNIS EQUIPMENT WALL RACK

This is an attractive way for the tennis athlete in your family to display his or her equipment and have it handy at the same time. The nameplate will clarify ownership for each tennis player in the family.

Materials

> **#10 plastic canvas** cut as follows:
> Nameplate: 1 piece 31 threads high × 81 threads wide for a 5-letter name. Adjust for a longer name.
> Ball can holder: 1 piece 39 threads × 92 threads and one 3"-diameter circle
> **Mounting board:**
> 1" × 6" × 20" pinewood
> wood dowels—¼" × 2" long
> stain or paint
> 3 or 4 flathead nails or staples
> white glue
> 4 decorative head nails
> **Yarn** DMC® Floralia® 3-ply Persian:
> Navy blue—6 yards
> White—20 yards
> **#20 tapestry needle**

Preparation

Cut the canvas to the sizes given. Note that the name shown has five letters. If your name is longer or shorter, adjust the length of the canvas to fit. The length of the mounting board may also have to be lengthened.

Stitching

Following your chosen name chart (see alphabets, pages 191–192), stitch the nameplate using the Continental stitch (page 144).

Leave 2 canvas threads unworked all around the perimeter for later finishing with the binding stitch.

Stitch the ball can holder using your initial or other motif. Leave 2 canvas threads unworked on the top long edge for later finishing with the binding stitch and 1 canvas thread at the bottom long edge and the two short sides for joining. Stitch the plastic circle for the can holder bottom.

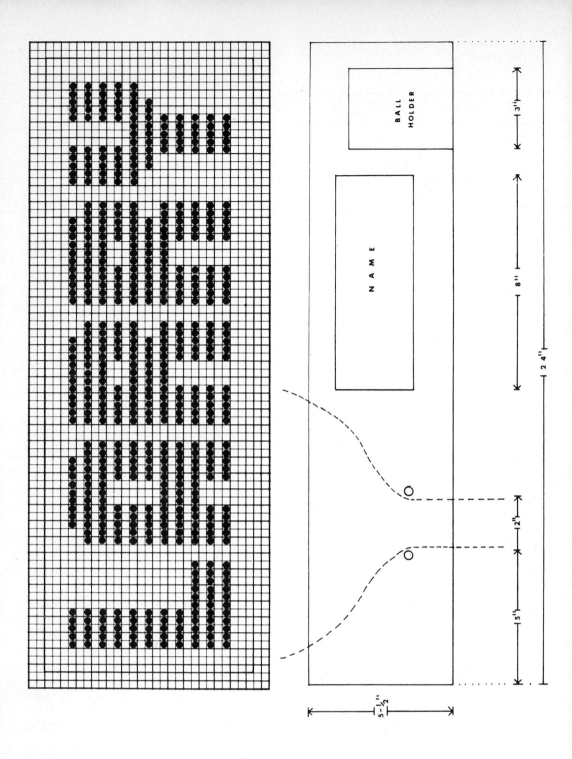

Finishing

Work the Binding Stitch (page 11) all around the perimeter of the nameplate.

Finish the ball can holder as described in Soda/Beer Can Cover, page 180.

Sand the mounting board, stain or paint the wood, and drill 2 holes to receive the dowels as shown on the chart. Glue the dowels in place.

Attach the nameplate with glue or 4 decorative head nails at the corners. The ball can holder is attached to the mounting board with 3 or 4 small flat-head nails or staples.

Stitched by Larry Berger.
Woodwork by Richard Schulman.
See color photograph.

TISSUE BOX COVER

This simple gingham check tissue box cover will dress up any dull bathroom or night table. Using the same pattern and a solid top, you can make this into a cover for a roll of bathroom tissue.

Materials

#7 plastic canvas cut as follows:
Top: 1 piece 30 threads × 30 threads
Sides: 4 pieces 30 threads × 38 threads
#18 tapestry needle
Yarn DMC® Floralia® 3-ply Persian:
White—5 skeins
Gray—5 skeins
Black—6 skeins

Preparation

Cut the canvas pieces to the sizes given. Carefully cut out the opening at the top with a crafts knife.

Stitching

Using 3-ply yarn, follow the diagram and stitch the gingham pattern in the Scotch stitch (page 130). The initial is optional and can be added as desired.
　　Remember to leave 1 thread *unworked* on all four sides of each piece for binding and joining.

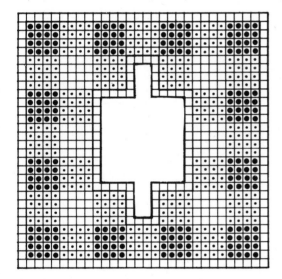

Finishing

First, join the four sides along the long edge using the Binding Stitch (page 11). Next, work the binding stitch around the cutout on the top piece. Then join it to the sides, again with the binding stitch.
　　See color photograph.

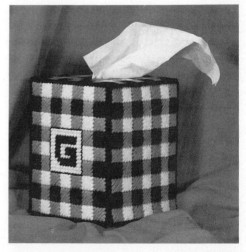

VISOR

This visor is worn in many sports to protect the eyes from glare and sunlight. In addition, this needlepointed sample has a terrycloth lining in the headband to act like a sweatband.

Materials

> **#10 plastic canvas** cut as follows:
>> Peak: 1 piece 62 threads × 94 threads
>> Headband: 1 piece 24 threads × 268 threads
> **#18 tapestry needle**
> **Yarn** DMC® Floralia® 3-ply Persian:
>> Royal blue—5 yards
>> Light blue—30 yards
> **Velcro®** ⅝″ × 2½″
> **Terrycloth for lining** 3″ × 25″
> **Lamp cord wire** 2′

Preparation

Cut the canvas to the sizes given.

Stitching

Using 2-ply Persian yarn and the Continental stitch (page 144), stitch the net design as shown on the diagram. Stitch the motif (tennis player) using 1-ply yarn with a backstitch, following the graph.
   Leave 1 canvas thread unworked around all edges for joining and finishing.

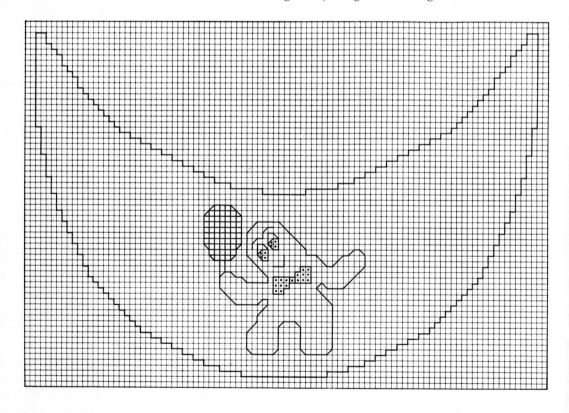

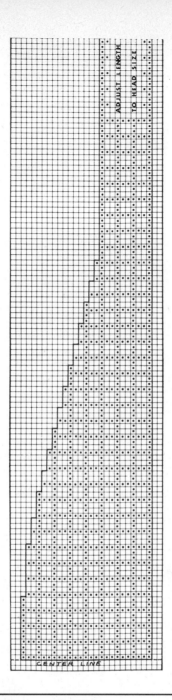

ADJUST LENGTH

TO HEAD SIZE

CENTER LINE

Finishing

Work the Binding Stitch (page 11) over 1 thread on the straight edge of the headband piece.

To attach the wire to the peak, lay the wire over the unworked thread around the curved edge. Using the binding stitch with 3-ply yarn, go over the wire and through the canvas. When finished, snip the wire to fit. Stitch over the wire ends a few times to keep them from moving.

To join the peak to the headband, match the center of the inside curve of the peak to the center of the straight edge of the headband. Join with the binding stitch.

Attach Velcro® to the ends of the headband with glue or slip-stitching. Using the headband as a pattern, cut a piece of terrycloth ¼" larger than the canvas. Turn the raw edges under ¼" and pin in place. Slip-stitch to the edges.

See color photograph.

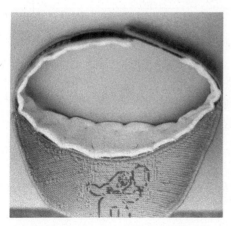

Finishing Touches

CARE AND FINISHING

BLOCKING

Most diagonal stitches will distort the canvas if you do not stitch on a frame. Even if you have used a frame, some stitches will distort the canvas. Blocking is the procedure used to correct this distortion.

It is not difficult to block a piece of needlepoint. The canvas is dampened, stretched back to its original shape, pinned to a board or frame, redampened, and allowed to dry slowly.

Step 1
Either buy a blocking board, make one from a piece of particle board (available from a lumber yard or home improvement center), or use a frame-type product meant for this purpose such as Marie Products® Easy Blocker. (See "Tools and Accessories," page 1.)

Step 2
Cover the board with a prewashed fabric. Gingham check is a good choice because the checks form a squared or graphlike surface that can be used to align and square up the canvas.

Step 3
Place the canvas (right side up) on the fabric-covered board. Using *rustproof* pins, tacks, or staples, secure the canvas to the board, starting at the center of each of the four sides. Work outward toward the corners, pulling the canvas as necessary to restore it to the original size and shape.

Step 4
Dampen the canvas with a spray mister or wet towel. At this point you can either let the canvas air-dry for 24–48 hours or use a steam iron held slightly *above* the surface of the work. *Do not let the iron rest on the canvas.* It would flatten the stitches and could damage the yarn or other fibers.

Another product that will assist and speed up your blocking is Marie's Canvas Spray 'N Block™. This is a professional blocking solution that is sprayed on the canvas to reduce blocking time to about 60 minutes. It is safe for colorfast materials (always make your own test).

FRAMING AND FINISHING

I always recommend using professional framers and finishers whenever possible. They have the expertise and equipment to correct severely distorted canvases, sew through thick fabric and canvas, and generally enhance the appearance of your work.

If you choose to frame a piece of needlepoint yourself, always remember to use spacers (fillets) between the glass and the needlepoint canvas to keep the glass from resting on the stitches and flattening them. Also remember that canvas and yarns will deteriorate if they cannot "breathe."

CLEANING

If the yarns or other fibers are colorfast, you can wash a dirty piece of needlework using a product specifically formulated for the cleaning of needlework such as Mountain Mist® Ensure.

If the yarns or fibers are not colorfast, they can be dry-cleaned. Do not let the cleaner steam the work—steaming can flatten the stitches.

STORAGE

Needlepoint work or materials (canvas and fibers) should *never* be stored in sealed plastic bags. If your work cannot "breathe," the canvas and yarns will discolor or even deteriorate.

For work in progress, I recommend covering and storing the piece in a *cotton* pillowcase.

Alphabets

The following alphabets were used to work many of the projects (see color insert) in this book.

The 5 × 5 alphabet can be used for writing a word or sentence, or for signing your finished needlework.

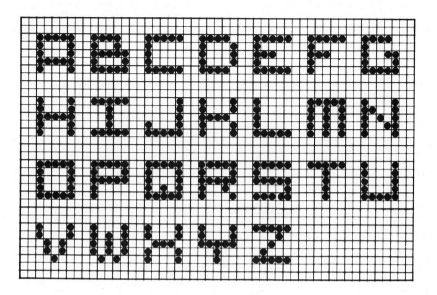

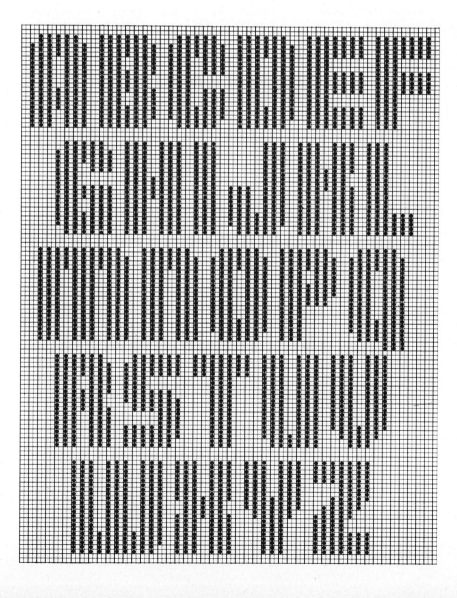

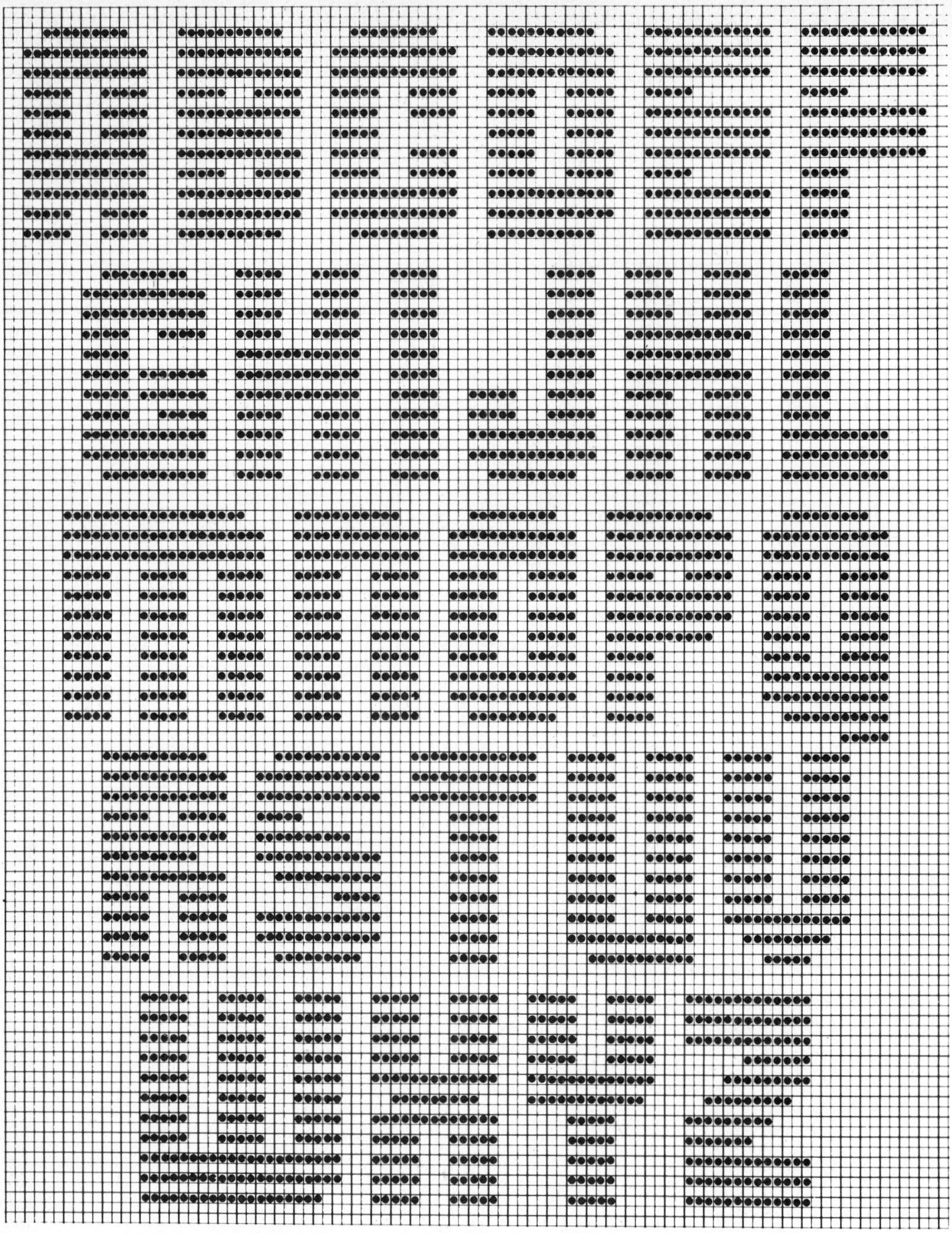

Bibliography

SELECTED BIBLIOGRAPHY

Ambuter, Carolyn. *Complete Book of Needlepoint.* New York: Thomas Y. Crowell, 1972

Christensen, Jo Ippolito. *The Needlepoint Book.* Englewood Cliffs, N.J.: Prentice-Hall, Inc., 1979

Eaton, Jan. *The Complete Stitch Encyclopedia.* London: Quarto Publishing Ltd., 1987

Fisher, Pauline, and Anabel Lasker. *Bargello Magic.* New York: Holt, Rinehart and Winston, 1972.

Hanley, Hope. *101 Needlepoint Stitches.* New York: Dover Publications, Inc., 1986

Harlow, Eve. *The New Anchor Book of Canvaswork Stitches & Patterns.* London: David and Charles, 1991

Hilton, Jean. *Needlepoint Stitches.* Westminster, Calif.: Published by the Author, 1988

Hilton, Jean. *Stimulating Stitches.* Flint, Mich.: Published by the Author, 1992

Rhodes, Mary. *Dictionary of Canvas Work Stitches.* New York: Charles Scribner's Sons, 1980

Rome, Carol Cheney, and Georgia French Devlin. *A New Look at Needlepoint.* New York: Crown Publishers, Inc., 1973

Zimmerman, Jane D. *The Canvas Work Encyclopedia.* Richmond, Calif.: Published by the Author, 1989

Index of Stitches

A

ALGERIAN EYE 23
ALGERIAN EYE, DOUBLE 23
ALGERIAN EYE, ELONGATED 24
ALGERIAN FILLING 24
ALICIA LACE 25
amadeus 81
ARROWHEAD 25
ARROWHEAD FLY 26

B

back 26
BACKSTITCH 26
bamboo 31
bamboo pattern 32
BARGELLO, SPLIT 26
BARGELLO WAVE PATTERN 27
BARRED SQUARE 28
BASKET 28
basket filling 28
basketweave 144
BAZAAR 29
BEETLE 29
BEETLE, BARRED 30
BINDING STITCH 11
BOKHARA COUCHING, RANDOM 31
BOKHARA COUCHING, STRIPE PATTERN 32
BOKHARA COUCHING, TIED 32
BOWTIE 32
BRICK 33
BRICK, DOUBLE 33
BRICK FILLING 34
BRICK, GIANT 34
BRICKING 34
BULLION KNOT 35
broad cross 28
BUTTONHOLE 36
BYZANTINE 36
BYZANTINE, GRADUATED 37
BYZANTINE SCOTCH 38

C

CASHMERE 39
CASHMERE, CHECKER 39
CASHMERE, DIAGONAL 40
CASHMERE, ELONGATED 40
CASHMERE, FRAMED 41
CASHMERE, TIED 41
CHAIN 42
CHAIN, DETACHED 42
CHECKER, LARGE 42
CHECKER, SMALL 43
chequer 42
chessboard 115
CHINESE 43
CHINESE KNOT 44
continental 144
continuous cashmere 40
CRISSCROSS 44
CROSS 45
CROSS, BRAIDED 46
CROSS, DIAGONAL UPRIGHT 46
CROSS, DOUBLE PLAITED 47
CROSS, HITCHED 48
CROSS, HOURGLASS 48
CROSS, OVERLAPPED OBLONG 49
CROSS, PLAITED 49

CROSS, ROMAN 50
CROSS, UPRIGHT 50
CROSS, WOVEN 51
CROSS AND HALF-CROSS VARIATION #1 51
CROSS AND HALF-CROSS VARIATION #2 51
CROSS AND HALF-CROSS VARIATION #3 52
CROSS I, BOUND 52
CROSS II, BOUND 53
crossed corners 123
CROSSED CROSSES 53
CROSSED DIAMOND 54
crossed straight 76
CROSSES, STAGGERED 54
CROW'S FOOT 55
cushion 130
cushion, alternating 130
cushion, cross-cornered 131
cushion, framed 132
cushion, reversed 130
cushion variation 130

D

DAISIES, SQUARED 55
DAMASK 56
DAMASK DARNING 57
DAMASK DARNING WITH CROSS 58
Darmstadt pattern 58
DARMSTADT PAVILION 58
diagonal 77
diagonal star 60
DIAMOND, STRAIGHT 59
DIAMOND EYE 60
diamond eyelet 60
DIAMOND RAY 60
diamond with backstitch 146
DOUBLE 61
double back 97
double cross 137
DOUBLE CROSS, TRAME 61
double tie-down 71
DOUBLE LEVIATHAN 62
DUTCH 62

E

elongated crossed corners 108
ENGLISH 63
EYE 63
eyelet 55, 63
EYELET, REVERSED 64
EYELET, SIX-SIDED 64

F

FAN 65
fancy cross 53
FERN 65
FISHBONE 66
FISHBONE, HORIZONTAL 66
flame 67
flat 130
FLORAL 66
FLORENTINE FLAME 67
FLOWER 68
FLY 69
FOUR, THREE, TWO CROSS 69
FRAME 70

FRENCH 1 70
FRENCH 2 71
FRENCH, DIAGONAL 72
FRENCH KNOT 72
FRENCH KNOT WITH TAIL 73

G

German 104
GINGHAM 74
GINGHAM MOSAIC 74
GINGHAM SCOTCH 75
Gobelin droit 79
GOBELIN, CROSSED 76
GOBELIN, ENCROACHING 76
GOBELIN, INTERLOCKING 77
Gobelin, oblique 77
GOBELIN, SLANTING 1 77
GOBELIN, SLANTING 2 77
GOBELIN, SPLIT 78
Gobelin, straight 79
GOBELIN, TRAME 78
GOBELIN, UPRIGHT 79
Greek 97
GROUNDING, SMALL 79

H

half-cross 145
HERRINGBONE 80
HERRINGBONE, DOUBLE INTERLACED 80
HILTON AMADEUS 81
HILTON JESSICA 82
HILTON MISTAKE 83
HOUNDSTOOTH 84
HUNGARIAN 84
HUNGARIAN, DOUBLE 85
HUNGARIAN, GROUNDING 1 85
HUNGARIAN, GROUNDING 2 86
HUNGARIAN, HORIZONTAL 86

I

interlaced cross 87
interlacing 98
INTERWOVEN CROSS 87
irregular Byzantine 37
ITALIAN CROSS 87
Italian, two-sided 87

J

JACQUARD 88
Jessica 82

K

KALEM 88
KNITTED 89
knitting 88
knitting Gobelin 88
knitting tent 117

L

LAZY ROMAN II 89
LEAF 1 90
LEAF 2 90
LEAF 3 91
LEAF, CRETAN 92
LEAF 1, DIAGONAL 92
LEAF 2, DIAGONAL 93
LEAF, DIAMOND 93
LEAF, HERRINGBONE 94
LEAF, MEDALLION 94
LEAF, RAISED CLOSE HERRINGBONE 95

LEAF, ROUMANIAN 95
leviathan 137
LINEN 96
LINK, SURFACE 96
LINKED STEPPED 97
linked, half-drop 97
LONG-ARMED CROSS 97
long-arm Smyrna 136
long-legged cross 97
long oblique 140
LOZENGE SATIN 98

M

MALTESE CROSS 98
MILANESE 100
MILANESE, STRAIGHT 100
MILANESE PINWHEEL 101
MILANESE VARIATION 101
minileaf 127
mistake 83
Montenegrin cross 102
MONTENEGRIN 102
MOORISH 103
MOORISH, WIDE 103
MOSAIC 104
MOSAIC, CROSSED 104
MOSAIC, DIAGONAL 105
MOSAIC, REVERSED 105
MOSAIC STRIPE 106
MOSAIC TILE 106

N

Norwich 153

O

OBLONG CROSS 107
OBLONG CROSS WITH BACKSTITCH 107
OBLONG RICE 108
OCTAGON EYE 108
octagon eyelet 108
octagonal eye 108
ORIENTAL 109
outline 109
OUTLINE, WOVEN 109
OVERCAST STITCH 10

P

PALACE PATTERN 110
PARIS 110
PARISIAN 111
PARISIAN, DOUBLE 112
pavilion steps 149
PAVILION, TIED 112
PAVILION, TIED (WITH BACKSTITCH) 113
Pekinese 43
PETIT POINT 114
PINEAPPLE 114
PINEAPPLE, ALTERNATING 115
pineapple, half-drop 115
PINEAPPLE, STEPPED 115
pinwheel 101
plaited Gobelin 80
PORTUGUESE 116
Portuguese border 116
Portuguese filling 116
Portuguese knotted stem 116
PORTUGUESE STEM 116

R

ray 65
REP 117

reversed eye 64
REVERSED TENT 117
RHODES 118
RHODES, CROSSED CORNER 118
RHODES, DIAMOND 119
RHODES, HALF 119
RHODES, HALF HALF-DROP 120
RHODES, HEART 120
RHODES, OCTAGONAL 121
RHODES, TIED 121
RIBBED SQUARE 122
RIBBED SQUARE SPIDER 122
RICE 123
rice, elongated 108
rice, oblong 108
RICE, STRAIGHT 123
RICE, TRIPLE 124
RICKRACK 124
RIDGE 125
ringed square 122
ROCOCO 125
ROMAN II 126
ROMAN III 126
roman filling 146
ROSEBUD 127
ROUMANIAN COUCHING 127

S

satin 79
SATIN, PADDED 128
SATIN TRIANGLES 128
SATIN TRIANGLES VARIATION 129
SCOTCH 130
SCOTCH, ALTERNATING 130
SCOTCH, BORDERED ALTERNATING 131
SCOTCH, CROSS-CORNERED 131
SCOTCH, FRAMED 132
SCOTCH, FRAMED CHECKER 132
SCOTCH I, ALTERNATING 133
SCOTCH II, ALTERNATING 133
Scottish 130
SEVEN 134
sheaf 134, 154
shell 154
SHELL 134
SHELL, LOOPED 135
six-color herringbone 29
six-sided eye 64
SMYRNA, ALTERNATING 136
SMYRNA, LINKED 136
Smyrna, tied 136
SMYRNA, CROSS 137
SPRAT 137
SPRINGS 138
STAR, DOUBLE 139
STAR, FRAMED 139
star of Bethlehem 140
STAR, SLANTING 140
STEM 140
STEM, DIAGONAL 141
STEM VARIATION 1 141

stepped backstitch 160
steps 160
ST. GEORGE AND ST. ANDREW CROSS 142
STRAIGHT AND UPRIGHT CROSSES, LARGE 142
straight cross 50
SURREY 143

T

tailor tack 137
TENT, ALTERNATING 143
TENT, BASKETWEAVE 144
TENT, CONTINENTAL 144
TENT, HALF-CROSS 145
tent, reversed 117
TENT VARIATION 145
TIED DIAMONDS 146
tied pavilion 112
tied pavilion with backstitch 113
TIED STAR 146
TRIANGLE 147
triangular, two-sided 150
TRIPLE CROSS 148
TRIPLE TWIST 148
TUMBLING BLOCKS 149
TURKEY 150
Turkey Knot 150
TURKISH, TWO-SIDED 150
TWEED 151

U

upright 79

V

VANDYKE 152
VELVET 152
VICTORIAN, STEPPED 153

W

WAFFLE 153
WEB 154
wheat 154
WHEATSHEAF 154
WICKER 155
wicker 28
William and Mary 153
WINDMILL 156
WINDMILL, CROSS TIED 156
woven cross 87
WOVEN CROSS, ASKEW 157
WOVEN RIBBONS 157
WOVEN SQUARE 158
WOVEN TENT 158
WOVEN TRELLIS 159

Z

ZIGZAG 160

BARGELLO PATTERNS

Upright Gobelin 16, *17*
4-2 Pattern 16, *17*
4-1 Pattern 16, *17*
Bargello Pattern #1 (scallop, wave) 17
Bargello Pattern #2 (pomegranate) 18

Bargello Pattern #3 (pomegranate variation) 19
Bargello Pattern #4 (argyle) 20
Bargello Pattern #5 (woven, woven ribbons) 21
Bargello Pattern #6 (trees, lollipops) 22

Conversion Chart

LINEAR MEASURES

---

1 inch	2.54	centimeters
1 foot	0.3048	meters
1 yard	0.9144	meters

AREA MEASURES

---

1 square inch	6.4516	square centimeters
1 square foot	929.03	square centimeters
1 square yard	0.836	square meters